THE ZEN OF MUHAMMAD ALI
And Other Obsessions

Davis Miller is the author of *The Tao of Muhammad Ali* and *The Tao of Bruce Lee*. Miller's story, 'My Dinner with Ali', was judged by the Sunday Magazine Editors Association to be the best essay published in an American newspaper magazine in 1989 and in 1999 was judged by David Halberstam to be one of the best twenty pieces of sports writing of the twentieth century. 'My Dinner with Ali' has been anthologised in *The Best American Sports Writing of the Century* and in *The Muhammad Ali Reader*. Miller has written fiction and non-fiction for numerous magazines and newspapers, including *Esquire, Men's Journal, Rolling Stone, GQ, Arena, Independent on Sunday, Washington Post, Los Angeles Times, Chicago Tribune* and the *Louisville Courier-Journal*, among many others. His non-fiction short story, 'The Zen of Muhammad Ali', was nominated by the *Miami Herald* for the 1994 Pulitzer Prize for feature writing and was anthologised in *The Best American Sports Writing, 1994*. He has two children, Johanna and Isaac, and lives near Winston-Salem, North Carolina, where he was born.

www.geocities.com/taoofdavismiller

D1313330

ALSO BY DAVIS MILLER

The Tao of Muhammad Ali: a fathers and sons memoir
The Tao of Bruce Lee: a martial arts memoir

Praise for *The Tao of Muhammad Ali*

'Ranks among the best of contemporary American writing.'
Independent

'Nobody has ever written so purely about Ali before. Maybe
no one has ever written so purely about anyone.'
Los Angeles Times

'Miller is Ali's spiritual Boswell. A compelling, strange
and beautiful book.'
Daily Telegraph

'What brilliant stories these are! Davis Miller writes
profoundly and beautifully.'
Joyce Carol Oates

'Miller's astounding book, more in the tradition of
writers such as Tobias Wolff and Richard Ford than that
of mere biographies, is a seminal interpretation of fame,
how it affects both those who have it and those
who live in its shadow.'
Esquire

'Filled with the clarity of ordinary human experience.
Miller's best writing occurs when he recalls periods of his
life when Ali was not part of it, for example the buzz of
early journalistic successes or the sudden illness that took his
father's life. After all, the real Zen lesson to be learned from
a man like Ali, Miller argues, has nothing to do with
lionizing the mighty infallible heroes whom we aspire to be.
It is, instead, about living with the potent fallibility
of ourselves.'
Times Literary Supplement

Praise for *The Tao of Bruce Lee*

'A martial arts Nick Hornby, Miller bulks up with a
punishing regimen and reads everything he can by or about
Lee, discovering a personal philosophy that allows him to
grow as an adult and feel secure in himself. Miller is
illuminating about the ability to transform oneself no matter
what the circumstances.'
The Times

'This fantastic second book by Miller runs deeper than an
account of the author growing up as a 'karate kid' in the
1970s. It is equally a study of the nature and role of
the hero in popular culture, a poignant and unusual
coming-of-age story, and an informative and revelatory
biography of Bruce Lee.'
Booklist

'Miller continues to invent a powerful new form of writing.'
Toronto Star

'Bruce Lee freed Miller to transform himself from someone
his high school classmates called "Foetus", and shut inside
lockers for fun, into a sinewy, 140-pound kickboxer . . . In
the section solely about Lee, Miller usefully debunks myths
about the martial artist's life, and especially about his
strange death with his mistress.
San Francisco Chronicle

'Often poignant, always potent. Miller has created the place
where New Journalism comfortably collides with classic
reporting and timeless, sumptuous storytelling.'
Winston-Salem Journal

Davis Miller

THE ZEN OF MUHAMMAD ALI

And Other Obsessions

VINTAGE

Published by Vintage 2002

2 4 6 8 10 9 7 5 3

Copyright © Davis Miller 2002

Davis Miller has asserted his right under the Copyright, Designs and Patents Act 1988 to be identified as the author of this work

This book is sold subject to the condition that it shall not, by way of trade or otherwise, be lent, resold, hired out, or otherwise circulated without the publisher's prior consent in any form of binding or cover other than that in which it is published and without a similar condition including this condition being imposed on the subsequent purchaser

First published in Great Britain
by Vintage in 2002

Vintage
Random House, 20 Vauxhall Bridge Road,
London SW1V 2SA

Random House Australia (Pty) Limited
20 Alfred Street, Milsons Point, Sydney,
New South Wales 2061, Australia

Random House New Zealand Limited
18 Poland Road, Glenfield, Auckland 10, New Zealand

Random House South Africa (Pty) Limited
Endulini, 5A Jubilee Road, Parktown 2193, South Africa

Random House UK Limited Reg. No. 954009
www.randomhouse.co.uk

A CIP catalogue record for this book
is available from the British Library

ISBN 0 09 942952 7

Papers used by Random House UK Ltd are natural, recyclable products made from wood grown in sustainable forests. The manufacturing processes conform to the environmental regulations of the country of origin

Set in 10½/12 Sabon by SX Composing DTP, Rayleigh, Essex
Printed and bound in Great Britain by
Cox & Wyman Limited, Reading, Berkshire

Photograph of Davis Miller and Muhammad Ali
by Len Irish
Photograph of Davis Miller by Beth Phillips

For my teacher, my hero, my son
Isaac Lee Miller

Thank you to my editor and friend Will Sulkin
for seeing to it that this was a book worth publishing –
and then publishing it.

CONTENTS

AUTHOR'S NOTE

Ever since my first book, *The Tao of Muhammad Ali*, was published in 1997, readers have asked me time and again where to find the magazine stories on which that book was based. I can now suggest exactly where to look – at this volume. The first section of *The Zen of Muhammad Ali and Other Obsessions* comprises three of my Ali stories, as well as a new piece called 'The Yin and the Yang of Muhammad Ali'.

In addition, I've hand-picked seven directly and indirectly related stories, including an essay titled 'Bruce Lee, American' that helped inspire my second book, *The Tao of Bruce Lee*. The result is a volume about fighting – fighting of all kinds – public displays and personal struggles.

Recognising that many readers are intrigued by the particulars of how and why stories come to be written – and how they are expanded into books (and, in some cases, edited from book chapters into magazine pieces) – I've penned either opening or closing 'insider' comments on the writing process and on the origins and histories of these works. I hope that you'll enjoy *The Zen of Muhammad Ali and Other Obsessions*. In many ways, it is my personal favourite among my first three books.

PART ONE: ALI

MY DINNER WITH ALI

Louisville Courier-Journal, 8 January 1989; *Sport*, May 1989; *Winston-Salem Journal* and *Detroit Free Press*, June 1990; *The Muhammad Ali Reader* (1998); *The Best American Sports Writing of the Century* (1999).

I'D BEEN WAITING for years. When it finally happened, it wasn't what I'd expected. But he's been fooling many of us for most of our lives.

For six months, several friends had been trying to connect me with him at his farm in Michigan. When I finally got to see him, it wasn't in Michigan and I didn't have an appointment. I simply drove past his mother's house in Louisville.

It was mid-afternoon on Good Friday, 1 April, two days before Resurrection Day. A block-long white Winnebago with Virginia plates was parked out front. Though he hadn't often been in town lately, I knew it was his vehicle. I was sure it was him because I know his patterns and his style. Since 1962, when he has travelled unhurried in this country, he has preferred buses or recreational vehicles. And he owns a second farm in Virginia. The connections were obvious. Some people study faults in the earth's crust or the habits of storms or of galaxies, hoping to make some sense of the world and of their own lives. Others meditate on the life and work of one social movement or one man. Since I was eleven years old, I

3

have been a Muhammad Ali scholar.

I parked my car behind his Winnebago and grabbed a few old magazines and a special stack of papers I'd been storing under the front seat, waiting for the meeting with Ali I'd been certain would come. Like everyone else, I wondered in what shape I'd find The Champ. I'd heard all about his Parkinson's syndrome and had watched him stumble through the ropes when introduced at recent big fights. But when I thought of Ali, I remembered him as I'd seen him years before, when he was luminous.

I was in my early twenties, hoping to become a world champion kick-boxer. And I was fortunate enough to get to spar with him. Later, I wrote a couple of stories about the experience and had copies of those with me, hoping he'd sign them.

Yes, in those days he had shone. There was an aura of light and confidence around him. He had told the world of his importance: 'I am the centre of the universe,' he had said, and we almost believed him. But recent reports had Ali sounding like a turtle spilled on to his back, limbs pitiably thrashing air.

It was his brother Rahaman who opened the door. He saw the stack of papers and magazines under my arm, smiled an understanding smile, and said, 'He's out in the Winnebago. Just knock on the door. He'll be happy to sign those for you.'

Rahaman looked pretty much the way I remembered him, a little like a black, ageing Errol Flynn. There was no indication in his voice or on his face that I would find his brother less than healthy.

I crossed the yard, climbed the couple of steps on the side of the Winnebago, and prepared to knock. Ali opened the door before I got the chance. He is, of course, a huge man. His presence filled the doorway. He had to lean under the frame to see me.

I felt no nervousness. Ali's face, in many ways, is as familiar to me as my father's. His skin remained unmarked, his countenance had nearly perfect symmetry. Yet something was different: Ali was no longer the world's prettiest man. This was only partly related to his illness; it was mostly because he was heavier than he needed to be. He remained handsome, but in the way of a youngish grandad who tells stories about how he could have been a movie star, if he'd wanted.

'Come on in,' he said and waved me past. His voice had a gurgle to it, as if he needed to clear his throat. He offered a massive hand. His grip was not a grip at all – his touch was gentle, almost feminine. His palm was cool and uncalloused; his fingers were the long, tapered digits of a hypnotist; his knuckles large, slightly swollen and rough. They looked as if he had recently been punching the heavy bag.

He was dressed in white, all white: new leather tennis shoes, cotton socks, custom-tailored linen slacks, short-sleeved safari-style shirt crisp with starch. I told him I thought white was a better colour for him than the black he often wore those days.

He motioned for me to sit, but didn't speak. His mouth was tense at the corners; it looked like a kid's who has been forced by a parent or teacher to keep it closed. He slowly lowered himself into a chair beside the window. I took a seat across from him and laid my magazines on the table between us. He immediately picked them up, produced a pen and began signing. 'What's your name?' he asked, without looking up, and when I told him, he continued writing. His eyes were not glazed, as I'd read in newspaper accounts, but they looked tired. A wet cough rattled in his throat. His left hand had continuous tremors. In the silence around us, I felt a need to tell him some of the things I'd been wanting to say for years.

'Champ, you changed my life,' I said. It's true. 'When I was a kid, I was messed up, couldn't even talk to people.' He raised his eyes from an old healthy image of himself on a magazine cover. 'You made me believe I could do anything,' I continued.

He was watching me while I talked; not judging, just watching. I picked up a magazine from the stack in front of

5

him. 'This is a story I wrote about the ways you've influenced my life.'

'What's your name?' he asked again, this time looking right at me. I told him. He nodded. 'I'll finish signing these in a while,' he said. He put his pen on the table. 'Read me your story.'

'You have a good face,' he said when I was through. 'I like your face.'

He'd listened seriously as I'd read, laughing at funny lines and when I'd tried to imitate his voice. He had not been bored. It was a lot more than I could have expected.

'You ever seen any magic?' he asked. 'You like magic?'

'Not in years,' I said.

He stood and walked to the back of his RV. He moved mechanically. It was my great-grandfather's walk. He motioned for me to follow. There was a sad yet lovely, noble and intimate quality to his movements.

He did about ten tricks. The one that interested me the most required no props. It was a very simple deception. 'Watch my feet,' he said. He was standing maybe eight feet away, with his back to me and his arms perpendicular to his sides. Then he seemed to levitate about three inches off of the floor. He turned to me and in his thick, slow voice said, 'I'm a *baadd* niggah,' and gave me the old easy Ali smile.

I laughed and asked him to do it again; it was a good one. I thought I might like to try it myself, just as twenty years earlier I had stood in front of the mirror in my dad's hallway for hours, pushing my worm of a left arm out at the reflection, wishing mightily that I could replicate Ali's cobra jab. And I had found an old laundry bag, filled it with socks and rags, and hung it from a ceiling beam in the basement. I pushed my left hand into that twenty-pound marshmallow two hundred, three hundred, a thousand times a day, concentrating on speed. I strove to make my fists move more quickly than thought, as fast as ionised Minute Rice, and then I'd try to spring up on my toes, as I had watched Ali do: I would try to fly like Ali, bounding away from the bag and to my left.

After the levitation trick, Ali grabbed an empty plastic milk jug from beside a sink. He asked me to examine it. 'What if I make this jug rise up from the sink this high and sit there? Will you believe?'

'I'm not much of a believer these days, Champ,' I said.

'Watch,' he said, pointing at the plastic container, and taking three steps back. I was trying to see both the milk jug and Ali. He waved his hands a couple of times in front of his body, said, 'Arise, ghost, arise,' in a foggy-sounding voice. The plastic container did not move from the counter.

'April Fool's,' said Ali. We both chuckled and he walked over and slipped his arm around my shoulders.

He autographed the stories and wrote a note on a page of my book-length manuscript I asked him to take a look at. 'To Davis Miller, The Greatest Fan of All Times,' he wrote, 'From Muhammad Ali, King of Boxing.'

I felt my stories were finally complete, now that he'd confirmed their existence. He handed me the magazines and asked me into his mother's house. We left the Winnebago. I unlocked my car and leaned across the front seat, carefully placing the magazines and manuscript on the passenger's side, not wanting to take a chance on damaging them or leaving them behind. Abruptly, there was a chirping, insect-sounding noise in my ear. I jumped back, swatted the air, turned around. It had been Ali's hand. He was standing right behind me, still the practical joker.

'How'd you do that?' I wanted to know. It was a question I'd find myself asking several times that day.

He didn't answer, but raised both fists to shoulder height and motioned me out into the yard. We walked about five paces, I put up my hands, and he tossed a slow jab at me. I blocked and countered with my own. Many fighters and ex-fighters throw punches at each other or at the air or at whatever happens to be around. It's the way we play. Ali must still toss a hundred lefts a day. He and I had both thrown our shots a full half-foot away from the other, but my adrenal gland was pumping at high gear from being around Ali and my jab had come out fast – it had made the air sing. He slid back a half-step and took a serious look at me. A couple of kids were riding past on bikes; they recognised Ali and stopped.

'He doesn't understand I'm the greatest boxer of all times,' he yelled to the kids. He pulled his watch from his arm, stuck it in his trouser pocket. He'd get down to business now. He danced to his left a little, loosening up his legs. A couple minutes before, climbing down the steps of his RV, he'd moved so awkwardly he'd almost lost his balance. I'd wanted to give him a hand, but knew not to. I'd remembered seeing old Joe Louis 'escorted' in that fashion by lesser mortals, and I couldn't do that to Muhammad Ali. But now that Ali was on his toes and boxing, he was moving fairly fluidly.

He flung another jab in my direction, a second, a third. He wasn't one-fifth as fast as he had been in 1975, when I'd sparred with him, but his eyes were alert, shining like black electric marbles, and he saw everything and was real relaxed. That's precisely why old fighters keep making comebacks: we are more alive when boxing than at almost any other time. The grass around us was green and getting high; it would soon need its first cutting. A blue jay squawked from an oak to the left. Six robins roamed the yard. I instinctively blocked all three of his blows, then immediately felt guilty about it, like being fourteen years old and knowing for the first time that you can beat your dad at table tennis. I wished I could've stopped myself from slipping Ali's jabs, but I couldn't. Reflexive training runs faster and deeper than thought. I zipped a jab to his nose, one to his body, vaulted a straight right to his chin, and was dead certain all three would have scored – and scored clean. A couple cars stopped in front of the house. His mom's was on a corner lot. Three more were parked on the side.

'Check out the left,' a young-sounding voice said from somewhere. The owner of the voice was talking about my jab, not Ali's.

'He's in with the triple greatest of all times,' Ali was shouting. 'Gowna let him tire himself out. He'll get tired soon.'

I didn't, but pretended to, anyway. 'You're right, Champ,' I told him, dropping my hands. 'I'm thirty-five. Can't go like I used to.' I held my right hand to my chest, acting out of breath. I looked at Ali; his hand was in the exact same position. We were both smiling, but he was sizing me up a little.

'He got scared,' Ali shouted, conclusively. Onlookers laughed from their bicycles and car windows. Some blew their horns; one yelled, 'Hey, Champ.'

'Come on in the house,' he said softly in my ear. We walked toward the door, Ali in the lead, moving woodenly through new grass, while all around us people rolled up car windows and started their engines.

Ali's family easily accepted me. They were not surprised to have a visitor and handled me with ritualistic charm and grace. Rahaman told me to make myself at home, offered a root beer, went to get it. I took a seat on the sofa beside Ali's mother, Mrs Odessa Clay. Mrs Clay was in her early seventies, yet her face had few wrinkles. Short, her hair nearly as orange as a hazy Louisville sunset, she was freckled, fragile-looking, and pretty. Ali's face is shaped much like his mother's. When he was fighting she was quite heavy, but she had lost what looked to be about seventy-five pounds over the past ten years.

Mrs Clay was watching Oprah Winfrey on TV. Ali had disappeared from the room and I was wondering where he had gone. Rahaman brought the drink, a paper napkin and a coaster. Mrs Clay patted me on the hand. 'Don't worry,' she said. 'Ali hasn't left you. I'm sure he's just gone upstairs to say his prayers.'

I hadn't realised that my anxiety was showing. But Ali's mother had watched him bring home puppies many times during his forty-six years. Mrs Clay spoke carefully, with a mother's sweet sadness about her. The dignified clip to her voice must once have been affected, but after cometing all over the globe with Ali, it now sounded genuinely British and Virginian in its inflections.

'Have you met Lonnie, Ali's new wife?' she asked. 'He's known her since she was a baby. I'm so happy for him. She's my best friend's daughter, we used to all travel to his fights together. She's a smart girl, has a master's degree in business. She's so good to him, doesn't use him. He told me, "Mom, Lonnie's better to me than all the other three put together." She treats him so good. He needs somebody to take care of him.'

Just then, Ali came back to the room, carrying himself high and with stately dignity, though his footing was unsteady. He fell deep into a chair on the other side of the room.

'You tired, baby?' Mrs Clay asked.

'Tired, I'm always tired,' he said, then rubbed his face a couple times and closed his eyes.

He must have felt me watching or was simply conscious of someone other than family being in the room. His eyes weren't closed ten seconds before he shook himself awake, balled his hands into fists, and started making typical Ali faces and noises at me – grimacing, growling, other playful cartoon kid stuff. After a few seconds he asked, 'Y-y-you OK?' He was so difficult to understand that I didn't so much hear him as conjectured what he must have been saying. 'Y-y-you need anything? They takin' care of you?' I assured him that I was fine.

He made a loud clucking noise by pressing his tongue against the roof of his mouth and popping it forward.

Rahaman came quickly from the kitchen. Ali motioned him close and whispered in his ear. Rahaman went back to the kitchen. Ali turned to me. 'Come sit beside me,' he said, patting a bar stool to his right. He waited for me to take my place then said, 'You had any dinner? Sit and eat with me.'

'Can I use the phone? I need to call home and let my wife know.'

'You got kids?' he asked. I told him I had two. He asked how old. I told him the ages.

'They know me?' he asked.

'Even the three-year-old. He throws punches at the TV whenever I play your fights.'

He nodded, satisfied. 'Bring 'em over Sunday,' he said, matter-of-factly. 'I'll do my magic for 'em. Here's my mother's number. Be sure to phone first.'

I called Lyn and told her where I was and what I was doing. She didn't seem surprised. She asked me to pick up a gallon of milk on the way home. I knew she was excited for me but we had a lot of history, some of it rough, and she wouldn't show emotion in her voice simply because I was hanging out with my childhood idol. In September 1977, when Lyn and I were in college, we skipped class, took most of the money from our bank accounts, drove from North Carolina all the way to New York, and attended the Ali–Earnie Shavers bout at Madison Square Garden. For the rest of the year, we had to live off what little money I was able to make posing for anatomy drawings for art students and getting five cents for each soda bottle we picked up beside highways on Saturday and Sunday afternoons. But I bet she'd say it was worth it to have seen Ali in what we knew would be one of his last fights.

Rahaman brought two large bowls of chilli and two enormous slices of white bread from the kitchen. Ali and I sat at our chairs and ate. He put his face down close to the bowl and the food was gone. Three minutes tops. As I continued to eat, he spoke easily to me.

11

'Do you know how many people in the world would like to have the opportunity you're getting, how many would like to come into my house and spend the day with me?' he said. 'Haven't fought in seven years and still get over four hundred letters a week.'

I asked how people got his address.

'I don't know,' he answered. 'Sometimes they come addressed "Muhammad Ali, Los Angeles, California, USA". Don't have a house in LA no more, but the letters still get to me.

'I want to get me a place, a coffee shop, where I can give away free coffee and doughnuts and people can just sit around and talk, people of all races, and I can go and talk to people. Have some of my old robes and trunks and gloves around, show old fight films, call it "Ali's Place".'

'I'd call it "Ali's",' I said, not believing there would or ever could be such a place but enjoying sharing his dream with him. 'Just "Ali's", that's enough. People would know what it was.'

'"Ali's"?' he repeated, and his eyes focused inward, visualising the dream.

'Do you have copies of your fights?' I asked. He shook his head, no. 'Well, look,' I said, 'why don't I go to a video place and see if I can rent some and we can watch them tonight? Would you like that? You want to ride with me?'

'I'll drive,' he said.

There was a rubber monster mask in the Winnebago and I wore it on my hand on the way to the video shop, pressing it against the window at stop lights. A couple times people in cars saw the mask, then recognised Ali. Ali wears glasses when he reads and when he drives. When he saw someone looking at him, he carefully removed his glasses, placed them in his lap, made his hands into fists and put them beside his head.

Ali was the worst driver I'd ever ridden with – other than my alcoholic grandfather near the end of his life. Ali careened from lane to lane, sometimes riding down the middle of the highway, and he regularly switched lanes without looking or giving turn signals. I balled my fists in my lap and pretended to be relaxed. A group of teenage boys became infuriated when he pulled in front of their old beat-up Firebird and cut them off. Three of them leaned out the windows, shooting him the finger. Ali shot it back.

At the movie store, we rented a tape of his fights and interviews called *Ali: Skill, Brains and Guts*, produced and directed by Jimmy Jacobs, the handball champion, fight historian and Mike Tyson's co-manager. Jacobs had recently died of a degenerative illness. Ali hadn't known of Jacobs' death until I told him. 'He was a good man,' Ali said. His voice had that same quality that an older person who daily reads obituaries takes on.

I stopped by my car again on the way into Mrs Clay's house. There was one more picture I hoped Ali would sign, but earlier I'd felt I might be imposing on him. It was a classic headshot in a beautiful out-of-print biography by Wilfrid Sheed that featured hundreds of wonderfully reproduced colour plates. I grabbed the book from the car and followed Ali into the house.

When we were seated, I handed him the book and he signed the picture on the title page. I was about to ask if he'd mind autographing the photo I especially wanted, but he turned to page two, signed that picture, then the next page and the next. He continued to sign for probably forty-five minutes, writing notes about opponents, wives, parents, Elijah Muhammad, Howard Cosell, then passed the book to his mother and brother to sign a family portrait. Ali autographed nearly every photo in the book, pointing out special comments as he signed.

'Never done this before,' he said. 'Usually sign one or two pictures.'

He closed the book, looked at me dead level and held it out at arm's length with both hands. 'I'm givin' you somethin' very valuable,' he said, handing me the biography as if deeding me the Book of Life.

I stared at the book in my open palms and felt that I should say something, that I should thank him in some way. I carefully placed it on a table, shook my head slightly and cleared my throat, but found no words.

Excusing myself to the bathroom, I locked the door behind me. Ali's huge black dress shoes were beside the toilet. The toe of one had been crushed, the other was lying on its side. When I unlocked the door to leave, it wouldn't budge. I couldn't even turn the handle. I knocked, then again. There was laughter from the other room. I yanked fairly hard on the door a couple times. Nothing.

Finally, it easily opened. I caught a glimpse of Ali bounding into a side room to the right, laughing and high-stepping like some oversized, out-of-shape, Nubian leprechaun. I peeked around the corner into the room. He was standing with his back flat against the wall. He saw me, jumped from the room and began tickling me. Next thing I knew, he had me on the floor, balled-up in a foetal position, tears flowing down both sides of my face, laughing. Then he stopped tickling and I climbed to my feet.

Everybody kept laughing. Mrs Clay's face was round and wide with laughter. She looked like the mom of a leprechaun. 'What'd you think happened to the door?' Rahaman asked. I told him I figured it was Ali. 'Then why you turnin' red?' he wanted to know.

'It's not every day,' I said, 'that I go to Muhammad Ali's, he locks me in the bathroom, then tickles me into submission.' Everyone laughed again.

Suddenly I recognised the obvious, that all day I'd been acting like a teenage admirer again. And that Muhammad Ali had not lost perhaps his most significant talent – the ability to transport people past thoughts and words to a world of feeling and play. Being around Ali, or watching him perform on TV, has always made me feel genuinely childlike. I looked at his family: they were beaming – Ali still flipped their switches, too.

We finally slipped the Ali tape into the VCR. Rahaman brought everyone another root beer and we settled back to watch, Rahaman to my left, Ali beside me on the right, Mrs Clay beside Ali. The family's reactions to the tape were not dissimilar to those you or I would have looking at old home movies or high school annuals. Everyone sighed and their mouths arced at tender angles. 'Oh, look at Bundini,' Mrs Clay said, and, 'Hey, there's Otis,' Rahaman offered. Whenever there was film of Ali reciting verse, we'd all recite with him. 'Those were the days,' Rahaman said several times, to which Mrs Clay wistfully responded, 'Yes, yes, they were.' After a half-hour or so, she left the room. Rahaman continued to watch the tape with us for a while but then he left, too.

Then: it was just Ali and me. On the TV, it was 1963 and he was framed on the left by Jim Jacobs and on the right by Drew 'Bundini' Brown. 'They both dead now,' he said, acute awareness of his own mortality in his tone.

For a time he continued to smile at the old Ali on the screen, but eventually he lost interest in peering at distant mountains of his youth. 'Did my mom go upstairs? Do you know?' he asked.

'Yeah, I think she's probably asleep.'

He nodded, stood and left the room. When he came back, he was moving heavily. His shoulder hit the frame of the doorway to the kitchen. He went in and brought out two fistfuls of cookies. Crumbs were all over his mouth. He sat beside me on the sofa. Our knees were touching. Usually when a man gets this close I pull away. He offered me a couple cookies. When he was through eating, he yawned a giant's yawn, closed his eyes, and seemed to go dead asleep.

'Champ, you want me to leave?' I said. 'Am I keeping you up?'

He slowly opened his eyes and was back to our side of the Great Mystery. The pores on his face suddenly looked huge, his countenance elongated, distorted, like that of someone in an El Greco. He rubbed his face the way I rub mine when I haven't shaved in a week.

'No, stay,' he said. His voice was very gentle.

'You'd let me know if I was staying too late?'

'I go to bed at eleven,' he said.

With the volume turned this low on the TV, you could hear the videotape's steady whirr. 'Can I ask a serious question?' I said. He nodded OK.

'You're still a great man, Champ, I see that. But a lot of people think your mind is fried. Does that bother you?'

He didn't hesitate before answering. 'No, there are ignorant people everywhere. Even educated people can be ignorant.'

'Does it bother you that you're a great man not being allowed to be great?'

'Wh-wh-whatcha mean, "not allowed to be great"?' he said, his voice barely finding its way from his body.

'I mean . . . let me think about what I mean . . . I mean the things you seem to care most about, the things the rest of us think of as *being* Muhammad Ali, those are exactly the things that have been taken from you. It just doesn't seem fair.'

'You don't question God,' he said.

'OK, I respect that, but . . . Aw, man, I don't have any business talking to you about this.'

'No, no, go on,' he said.

'It just bothers me,' I said. I was thinking about the obvious ironies, thinking about Ali continuing to invent, and be invented by, his own mythology. About how he used to talk more easily, maybe better, than anybody else in the world; how he still thinks with speed and dazzle, but it takes serious effort for him to communicate even with people close to him. About how he may have been the world's best athlete – when walking he had the grace of a cat turning a corner; now, at night, he stumbles around the house. About how it's his left

16

hand, the most visible phenomenon of his boxing greatness, the hand that dominated more than 150 sanctioned fights and countless sparring sessions, *it's his left hand*, not the right, that shakes almost continuously. And I was thinking how his major source of pride, his 'prettiness', remains more or less intact. If Ali lost thirty pounds, he would still look classically Greek. Despite not expecting to encounter the miraculous any more than any other agnostic, I was sort of spooked by the seeming precision with which things have been excised from Ali's life.

'I know why this has happened,' Ali said. 'God is showing me, and showing you' – he pointed his trembling index finger at me and widened his eyes – 'that I'm just a man, just like everybody else.'

We sat a long quiet time then, and watched Ali's flickering image on the television screen. It was now 1971 and there was footage of him training for the first Joe Frazier fight. Our Most Public Figure was then The World's Most Beautiful Man and The Greatest Athlete of All Time, his tight copper-coloured skin glowing under the fluorescents, secret rhythms springing in loose firmness from his fingertips.

'Champ, I think it's time for me to go,' I say and make an effort to stand.

'No, stay. You my man,' he says and pats my leg. I take his accolade as the greatest compliment of my life.

'I'll tell you a secret,' he says and leans close. 'I'm gowna make a comeback.'

'What?' I think he's joking, hope he is, but something in the way he's speaking makes me uncertain. 'You're not serious.'

And suddenly there is musk in his voice. 'I'm gowna make a comeback,' he repeats louder, more firmly.

'Are you serious?'

'The timing is perfect. They'd think it was a miracle, wouldn't they?' He's speaking in a distinct, familiar voice; he's easy to understand. It's almost the voice I remember from when I first met him in 1975, the one that seemed to come roiling up from down in his belly. In short, Ali sounds like Ali.

'Wouldn't they?' he asks again.

'It would be a miracle,' I say.

'Nobody'll take me serious. But then I'll get my weight down to two-fifteen and have an exhibition at Yankee Stadium or someplace. Then they'll believe. I'll fight for the title. It'll be bigger than the Resurrection.' He stands and walks to the centre of the room.

'It'd be good for you to get your weight down,' I say.

'Watch this,' he says and dances to his left. He's watching himself in the mirror above the TV. His clean white shoes bounce smoothly around the room; I marvel at how easily he moves. His white clothing accentuates his movements in the dark room. The white appears to make him glow. He starts throwing punches, not the kind he'd tossed at me earlier, but now really letting them zing. I'd thought that what he'd thrown in the yard was indicative of what he had left. But what he'd done was allow me to play; he'd wanted me to enjoy myself.

'Look at the TV. That's 1971 and I'm just as fast now.' It's true, the old man can still do it. He can still make fire appear in the air. One second, two seconds, ten punches flash in the night. He looks faster standing in front of me than the ghostlike Ali images on the screen do. God, I wish I had a video camera to tape this. Nobody would believe me.

'And I'll be even faster when I get my weight down.'

'You know more now, too,' I find myself admitting. Jesus, what am I saying? And why am I saying this?

'Do you believe?' he asks.

'Well . . .' I say. The Parkinson's is affecting his sanity. Look at the grey shining in his hair.

And Ali throws another three dozen blows at the gods of mortality – he springs a triple hook off of a jab, drops straight right leads in multiples, explodes into a blur of uppercuts, and the air pops, and his fists and feet whirr. This is his best work. His highest art. When Ali was fighting, he typically held back a little; this is the stuff he seldom chose, or had, to use against opponents.

18

'Do you believe?' he asks, breathing hard, but no harder than I would if I'd thrown the number of punches he's just thrown.

They wouldn't let you, even if you could do it, I'm thinking. There's so much concern everywhere for your health. Everybody thinks they see old Mr Thanatos calling you.

'Do you believe?' he asks again.

'I believe,' I hear myself say.

He stops dancing and points a magician's finger at me. Then I get the look, the smile, that has closed one hundred thousand interviews. 'April Fool's,' he says and sits down hard beside me again.

We sit in silence for several minutes. I look at my watch. It's eleven eighteen. I hadn't realised it was that late. I'd told Lyn I'd be in by eight.

'Champ, I better go home. I have a wife and kids waiting.'

'OK,' he says almost inaudibly and yawns the sort of long uncovered yawn people usually do among family.

He's bone-tired, I'm tired, too, but I want to leave him by saying something that will mean something to him, something that will set me apart from the two billion other people he's met, that will imprint me indelibly in his memory and will make the kind of impact on his life he has made on mine. I want to say the words that will cure his Parkinson's.

Instead I say, 'We'll see you Easter, Champ.'

He coughs and gives me his hand. 'Be cool and look out for the ladies.' His words are so volumeless and full of fluid that I don't realise what he's said until I'm halfway out the door.

I don't recall picking up the book he signed, but I must have; it's sitting beside my typewriter now. I can't remember walking across his mom's yard and don't remember starting the car.

I didn't forget Lyn's gallon of milk. The doors to the grocery store whooshed closed behind me. For this time of

19

night, there were quite a few customers in the store. They seemed to move more as floating shadows than as people. An old feeling came across me that I immediately recognised. The sensation was much like going out into the day-to-day world shortly after making love for the first-ever time. It was that same sense of having landed in a lesser reality. And of having a secret that the rest of the world can't see. I'd have to wake Lyn and share the memory of this feeling with her.

I reached to grab a jug of milk and caught a reflection of myself in the chrome at the dairy counter. There was a half-smile on my face and I hadn't realised it.

'My Dinner with Ali' was my first major publication and also my first, and still most famous, essay. I feel obliged to thank the previously uncredited co-author of this story – Aaron Copland. 'My Dinner with Ali' was inspired by, and modelled after, three Copland works, including Appalachian Spring, Letter from Home, *and 'The Promise of Living' movement of his orchestral suite from* The Tender Land.

THE ZEN OF MUHAMMAD ALI

Esquire, September 1992; *Playboy* (Japan and Germany), March 1994; *Penthouse* (South Africa), July 1994; cover story in 1993 and early 1994 for newspaper magazines published by *Miami Herald*, *Chicago Tribune*, *Louisville Courier-Journal*, *Pittsburgh Post-Gazette*, *Cleveland Plain Dealer*, *Independent on Sunday*, *Melbourne Age*, *Detroit Free Press*, *Dallas Morning News*, *Buffalo News*, New York *Newsday* and *Denver Post*; cover piece for features sections of numerous newspapers, including *Washington Post*, *Houston Chronicle*, *Seattle Times*, *Winston-Salem Journal*, *Toledo Blade*, *South Ireland Independent*, *Sydney Morning Herald*, *Grand Rapids Press*, *Indianapolis Star* and *Folha de São Paulo* (Brazil); also published in *The Best American Sports Writing 1994*.

IN A SUITE on the twenty-fourth floor of the Mirage Hotel, Muhammad Ali is sitting on a small white sofa near full-length windows that overlook much of the east side of Las Vegas. He's wearing a pair of well-pressed, dark pinstripe slacks and a white, V-neck T-shirt that has a couple of nickel-sized holes in it, one of which reveals whorls of thin white hair on the left side of his chest. His waist is very thick; I'd guess he weighs about 265. 'My man,' he says. 'Glad to see you.'

Ali and I go back a long way. I first became a serious Ali

watcher in January 1964. I was eleven years old and was the shortest and skinniest and sickliest kid in town. My mother had died unexpectedly only a few months before. Her death had hit me hard. I'd been in and out of hospital, where I'd been pumped full of glucose and fluids because I'd refused to eat. At home, I spent nearly every waking moment staring at the TV. I talked occasionally to my father and less to my sister, but I was mostly silent.

Ali was still Cassius Clay. He'd just turned twenty-two and was luminous as he prepared to meet Sonny Liston for the biggest prize in sport, the world heavyweight championship. I remember sitting mesmerised in front of my dad's small black-and-white television as Ali's voice roared from the huge world outside and through the TV's rattling three-inch speaker. 'I'm young and handsome and fast and pretty and can't possibly be beat,' the voice said. And the voice touched radium in me.

I recall standing in front of the full-length mirror in the hall bathroom for hours at a time after that, pushing my worm of a left arm out at the reflection, trying feebly to imitate Ali's cobra jab. And my dad took an old laundry bag, filled it with rags and hung it from a ceiling beam in the basement. I pushed my fists into that twenty-pound marshmallow two hundred, five hundred, a thousand times a day, concentrating on speed: dazzling, crackling speed, in pursuit of godly speed; I strove to make my fists move more quickly than thought (like Ali's), and I tried to spring up on my toes, as I had watched Ali do; I tried to fly like Ali, bouncing around the bag and to my left.

Since then, many of the events that have defined my life have been related to Ali.

While in college, my first ever story for a national magazine was about another of my seminal Ali experiences – a sparring session I'd had with The Champ in 1975, when, largely because of his influence, I was trying to make a living as a kickboxer. In September 1977, my girlfriend and I eloped and tried (unsuccessfully) to get married at the Ali–Earnie Shavers bout. But by 1986, when I became the district manager of a video shop chain in Ali's hometown of Louisville, I seldom thought about him. He had been a childhood obsession.

While driving to one of the video stores, a friend who was with me pointed across the street and said, 'Muhammad Ali's mom lives there.' From then on, I radared in on the house whenever I passed by. On the Friday before Easter 1989, a block-long white Winnebago was parked out front. The license plate read 'THE GREATEST'.

I parked, worked up courage, walked to the house. Ali's brother Rahaman opened the door. He smiled – this was something he'd seen hundreds of times. He said, 'He's out in the Winnebago. Go knock on the door.' When I did, Ali asked me in, did magic tricks, invited me to stay for dinner.

I've seen a lot of Ali since that day. Recently, I've written several pieces about him, including one about that first meeting that won several awards. Because of Ali, after nearly ten years of trying, I am finally able to eke out a living as a writer.

Now, at the Mirage, Ali stands and steps stiffly to the picture windows that overlook Las Vegas. He motions for me to follow. 'Look at this place,' he says, scarcely louder than a whisper. 'This big hotel, this town. It's dust, all dust.' His voice is so volumeless that the words seem to be spoken not by Ali, but by a spectre standing in his shadow. 'Don't none of it mean nothin'. It's all only dust.'

We stare down at the sun-bleached town. In the middle distance, before the edge of the Spring Mountain range, an F-15 touches down at Nellis Air Force Base. 'Go up in an airplane,' Ali is saying, his voice sounding full of phlegm and ether. 'Go high enough and it's like we don't even exist. I've been everywhere in the world, seen everything, had everything a man can have. Don't none of it mean shit.' His tone is not cynical; indeed, it is almost hopeful.

He shuffles awkwardly back to the sofa and drops heavily on to his seat. Ali himself admits that the Parkinson's

23

syndrome that has shaken his body and thickened his speech was brought on by blows he suffered in the ring. He shows little bitterness.

'The only thing that matters is submitting to the will of God,' he says. 'The only things you've got is what's been given to you.'

He gestures for me to join him by patting the cushion to his left. 'How you been?' he asks.

'I'm OK,' I say. 'But my dad died a couple months ago.'

This surprises The Champ. He turns and looks at me so empathetically you'd think we shared the same parentage. 'How old was he?' he asks.

'Only fifty-nine. And I thought he was healthy. He was getting ready to retire and I thought I'd have lots of time with him. He was both my father and my mother.'

'How'd he pass?' Ali asks. 'A heart attack?'

I nod yes. Ali pats me on the hand. 'I know you miss him,' he says. 'When I first won the title, people used to call me up, messin' with me, tell me my father'd been killed. Used to scare me so bad. Life is so, so short. Bible says it's like a vapour.'

He picks up the TV's remote control from the sofa's armrest and tours the channels, stopping on a music network that's playing an old Michael Jackson song. He turns off the sound; we watch.

'Gandhi,' he says, as the Indian spiritual leader's grey ghostlike image flashes on to the screen. 'Mother Teresa,' a few seconds later. It's obvious that Ali feels a kinship with the faces and their deeds. Images matter to Ali. He intones the names as if they were incantatory.

He puts down the remote, moves mechanically for the bathroom, and when he gets there, slowly takes a white, starch-crisp shirt from its hanger on the door and slips it on, then struggles a little with the buttons. Without tucking the shirt in his trousers, he pulls a royal-red tie over his head that has been pre-knotted, I'm sure, by his wife Lonnie. He looks at me through the mirror and nods slightly, which I take to mean he'd like my help. In this moment, the most talented athlete of the twentieth century looks so eggshell fragile that I find my hands shaking a little. I might have imagined performing this service for my dad, had he lived to his seventies. Never for Muhammad Ali.

Ali is so large I have to stand on my toes to reach across the huge expanse of his back to slip the tie under his collar. He puts his shirt in his slacks without unsnapping or unzipping, then tugs on his jacket. Without being asked, I pick motes of white lint from the coat's dark surface and help him straighten his tie.

He picks up his briefcase and we leave the room. In the elevator, he says, 'Watch how people react.'

When we reach the ground floor, as the doors open he makes a loud clucking noise by popping his tongue forward across the roof of his mouth. The sound is quickly repeated from probably twenty feet away. Seconds later, Howard Bingham, who has been Ali's personal photographer and best friend for nearly thirty years, appears in the doorway. We walk from the elevator, Ali in the lead; Bingham follows me. Within moments, there are over a hundred people around us, wanting to touch Ali or shake his hand. Cameras appear from women's purses, as do pens and scraps of paper. 'Do the shuffle, Champ,' an older man shouts.

Ali hands me his briefcase, gets up on his toes and dances to his left. He tosses a few slow jabs at several people, then for a couple seconds allows his black shiny street dogs to blur into the patented Ali shuffle. The crowd, ever growing, explodes into laughter and applause. A space clears behind him and he uses it, knows it's there without turning to look. He moves toward the right corner of the wide hallway, waving on his audience, then turns to take his briefcase from me, which contains hundreds of yellow and green and blue Muslim pamphlets that have been personally signed by Ali and pre-dated with today's date. Bingham reappears with a metal folding chair. Ali sits, places the briefcase on his lap and produces an inexpensive pen from the pocket of his jacket.

Two minutes later, there is no way to skirt the throbbing crowd around Ali. There's every bit of five hundred people in the hallway. A Mirage security guard uses his walkie-talkie to call for reinforcements, and directs people who want autographs into a line.

I stand at Ali's right shoulder, against the wall. Bingham is to my left. We're in those exact positions for nearly an hour before I ask Bingham, 'Is it always like this?'

Ali's companion-photographer looks basically the way I recall from the seventies, a little hangjawed like the old MGM cartoon character Droopy. 'Always,' he says. 'Everywhere in the world. Last year, over 200,000 came to see him in Jakarta.'

'How long will he do this?' I want to know, meaning today.

Bingham shrugs. 'Until he gets tired. For hours. All day.'

Ali gives every waiting person something personal. He talks to almost no one, yet most everyone seems to understand what he means. He signs each person's first name on the Muslim literature and hugs, and is hugged by, everybody from three-year-old tykes to their eighty-year-plus great-grandmamas. He has a radar that is attuned to children. Whenever kids are near, he goes out of his way to pick them up and snuggle and kiss them, sometimes more tenderly than one could imagine their own parents doing. The first time I met him, one of the first questions he asked was if I had kids. I now want to know why he connects so to children.

'They're angels in exile,' he replies, speaking in the same tone you'd expect from a monk exposing the uninitiated to the mysteries. 'Children are so close to God. They haven't had time to separate from Him.'

Women and men in line openly weep upon seeing Ali. Many recount stories about his impact on their lives. Some tell of having met him years before. He often pretends to remember. A huge, rough-looking, Italian-American fellow in his mid-forties takes Ali's hand, kisses it, then refuses an autograph. 'I don't want anything from you, Champ,' he says. His mud-brown eyes are red and swollen. 'We've taken too much already.'

I have breakfast with Ali the next morning. He's wearing the same suit and tie. This is not a sign of financial need or that he doesn't remember to change clothes. Even when he was fighting, and making tens of millions of dollars, he didn't own more than a few suits. He's seldom worn jewellery and his watch is a Timex.

I ask why, unlike the old days, everyone, everywhere, seems to love him. 'Because I'm baadd,' he clowns, but then holds up his shaking left hand, spreads its fingers and says, 'It's because of this. I'm more human now. It's the God in people that connects them to me.'

At Miami International Airport, I unexpectedly run into Ali. As usual, he's at the centre of a crowd and people are looking at him with the same sweet sadness they ordinarily reserve for a favourite uncle who has recently suffered a stroke.

As always, he's not surprised to see me. He's wearing a black short-sleeved shirt, a pair of black dress trousers. He's carrying about a hundred of his Muslim handouts. His hair needs combing and his face is swollen. He looks exhausted.

'Been to see Angelo Dundee,' he tells me. 'Been travellin' too much. I'm tired of travellin'.'

I ask if he'd like a root beer. We walk a couple hundred yards to a coffee shop. A few people follow along until we go inside.

As we enter, he spots a woman with her head folded into her arms, slumped across a table. He takes a seat beside her and asks what's wrong. She looks up and doesn't seem to recognise Ali, but tells him that her purse has been stolen. The woman is short and dumpy, and she's wearing a pink warm-up suit.

She laughs wearily. 'It had all my money in it. I don't know how I'm going to get home. And how can I tell my husband? He doesn't like me spending so much, anyways. Sometimes we have some real blow-outs over money.'

Ali puts his pamphlets on the table and pulls a tattered brown cowhide wallet from his trousers pocket. It has $300 cash in it and an old picture of him with all eight of his kids. Although he's no longer world-class wealthy, he gives the woman $280.

The Champ greets me at the door to his mother's house in Louisville. It's very hot today, over 100. He's wearing a sky-blue safari suit and a pair of white tennis shoes. His face has lost much of its puffiness; his pecan-coloured skin refracts the late summer sun. In this moment, he looks much like the Ali we remember. 'Man, you look good. Are you working-out?' I ask.

'Doin' five rounds heavy bag, five speed bag, five shadow-boxin'. Lost over thirty pounds.'

I follow him to the kitchen and take a chair at a cream-coloured, Formica-topped dinette table. Cassius Clay Sr's stained and yellowed registration card for a 1972 Cadillac is propped between salt and pepper shakers. Ali's dad had died only a few months before. I pick up the paper and think about my father's social security card sitting on my desk at home.

'How do you feel?' I ask.

'Got more energy. Move better.'

Mrs Clay comes into the room. 'Oh, I'm so glad you're here,' she says to me. Like her son, Odessa Clay has a pretty, oval-shaped face. She's wearing a yellow paisley dress and she smells of flour. Although she seems tired and a light sweat shines on her forehead and neck, she smiles a fragile smile. 'Would you like a glass of root beer?' she asks.

She brings the soda in an old jelly glass. Ali leaves the room to say his midday prayers.

'These days,' I say, 'what does he talk about when it's just you and him?'

'Oh, he doesn't talk any more. He's so quiet you forget he's in the house. He writes and reads all the time. Reads and writes all day long.'

Ali returns to the kitchen, still barefoot from his prayers, moving so quietly I can't help but believe he's trying not to disturb even the dust beneath his feet. We go downstairs and sit side by side on the sofa. A gold-framed certificate I haven't seen before is hanging crooked above the TV. I get up to see what's on it. 'In Memoriam,' it reads, 'the Los Angeles County Board of Supervisors extends its deepest sympathy to you in the passing of your beloved father, Cassius Marcellus Clay.'

'It was a relief,' Ali says before I have a chance to ask. 'He was gettin' so old, in so much pain all the time. Talked to him a week before he died. He said he wouldn't see me again. "I'm tired," he said. "Tired of this pacemaker. Don't want it no more." It happens to all of us. It'll happen to me before long, it'll happen to you. We'll close our eyes and won't open them again. I'm preparing myself for the next life. That's what matters now.'

A few minutes later, he says, 'I'm tired. I need a nap. The heat's botherin' me.' The words sound ancient, totemic. 'Are you gowna be here when I wake up?' he asks.

'I think I'll go on home,' I tell him.

He reaches to hug me, all the time watching my eyes. His body is so thick, his skin cool and moist through the thin shirt. I remember rubbing my dad's back and shoulders in the hospital. Next Wednesday, it'll be exactly one year since he died. Ali's skin smells of earth and of trees. I kiss him on the cheek.

'Be cool and look out for the ladies,' he says. It is his standard way of saying goodbye.

*

Ali has been at a gym in Philadelphia, signing autographs for children. He's gained weight again. He's at probably 250, but he looks OK and his energy level is pretty good.

As we leave the gym, I slide into the limousine and take a seat across from him. An elderly man who looks a little like Ali's dead father startlingly appears beside the limo. He taps on my window with his left knuckles. I jump. 'Mr Clay, Mr Clay,' he shouts and offers Ali, a Muslim who never eats pork, a hot dog. The man is razor-thin, stubble-cheeked and his eyes are yellow with age, cheap wine and a life spent on street corners. Ali motions me to lower my window. He takes the old guy's hand for a moment. As we leave the kerb, I ask, 'Do you let everybody in?' I've never seen him refuse anyone.

'Don't want to disappoint nobody. But I try to be careful. There's a lot of crazy people out there. And a lot of people who hurt you without meanin' to.'

A couple minutes later, we pull up to a stop light. To my left, a heavy woman, dressed in browns and greys, who has no legs or hands, is propped against a doorway. She is playing 'Amazing Grace' on a harmonica that has been attached to her mouth by a strand of what looks to be plastic clothes line. 'We don't know how that lady got here,' Ali says. 'She's just like you and me.' As he says this, his left hand begins to dramatically tremble.

Ali closes his eyes, drops into a light sleep and begins to snore. Watching, I can't help but consider how the young Ali's seemingly endless energy had promised us that he would never get old. And how in many ways he is now older than just about anyone his age. But this is not sad. One of the first things one notices when spending serious time with Ali is that his life is still larger than that of anyone almost any of us has known. And that he seems less than fulfilled only when we see him in the smallest of ways, when we don't recognise that his Parkinson's syndrome and its aura of silence enlarges both his legend and his life. In a way, his silence helps him come off as something of a seer. As his health is deteriorating, he seems to be becoming a more spiritual being. Most of the time, he no longer aches with the ambition and the violence of a young god; some of his ego has thankfully been washed away.

I study the shape of his head, watch its almost perfect symmetry. He looks like a sleeping newborn, or a Buddha. Surely, his is an ancient soul. Maybe he's some kind of bodhisattva. And maybe he's also a little like Chance, the gardener, in Jerzy Kosinski's novel, *Being There* – a slate on to which we write what we wish, a screen on to which most anything can be projected – mysteries swirling through his life that appear to have meaning but which no one can quite explain.

There are around seventy-five noisy people at a Louisville gym. Almost none of them are boxers. Ali is dressed in a suit and tie and is playfully winging clownish punches at everybody around him. His moves come fairly loose and reasonably fast.

He turns and sees me and nods, then puts both hands beside his head. I get up on my skates and dance to my left, in exactly the style I'd learned from him twenty-five years before. He feigns surprise. 'I could be your daddy,' he says, 'if I was white.'

We pirouette around the old wooden floor for probably forty-five seconds, punching a half-foot from each other's chins and bodies. I find myself smiling. I feel good.

He points at a young blond amateur heavyweight, who looks like a fraternity kid. The Champ motions toward the ring and removes his jacket. I'm sure he must be joking, but he picks up a pair of licorice-coloured Everlasts and walks to the ring apron.

He pulls his tie from his neck and the sixteen-ounce sheaths of leather are strapped on his wrists. 'Gonna do five rounds,' he yells to the people gathering ringside. The volume level of his voice has greatly increased. And the sound no longer issues from high in his throat; there's a roundness to his words.

31

In his corner, a second pulls Ali's shirt-tail from his trousers; the top button remains buttoned. Someone says, 'Ding,' and then it's actually happening – sick old Muhammad Ali is really boxing.

I want to wince with each blow thrown. I feel a fat cockroach of sweat crawl down the small of my back. Ali doesn't seem able to get on his toes; his balance doesn't look good. He's throwing jabs, but every punch is missing. I believe the frat kid may be holding back in order to avoid hurting our ailing legend. But suddenly, around one minute into the round, The Champ drops his gloves to his sides, exposing his chin, and when his opponent tries to reach him with punches, he pulls his head back and away, just like the Ali we remember, causing the kid to miss by less than an inch.

At the beginning of Round Two, Ali's face is animated, focused, serious. The kid comes out hard, wanting to make it a real fight. He thumps Ali with stiff punches to the chin and to the chest. Ali covers up. The kid steps in and Ali stabs him with a well-timed jab that's as sweet as a bite from the last tangy apple of autumn. Fifteen seconds later, he shivers the college kid's legs with a straight right lead. At this, Ali backs off. He doesn't want to hurt his student. The kid gets on his bicycle; for a few moments he wears the expression of someone who has just been made aware of his own mortality. Ali continues to box the rest of the round at a level just slightly above the boy's abilities. With twenty seconds left, he zings in a series of eight jabs and a razor of a right, all designed to make only surface contact, but to confirm that he is still Ali.

The old master does three more rounds with less capable students than the frat kid, then he steps awkwardly from the ring and immediately begins his great-grandaddy walk.

He takes a seat with me on the edge of the ring. 'H-h-how did I look?' he asks. He has to repeat the question twice before I understand. Both of his arms are shaking, as is his head. 'D-d-did I surprise you?'

I admit that he did. He chuckles and nods, satisfied.

He pulls on his jacket and takes probably five minutes to knot his tie. We walk from the gym into a thin mist. The sidewalk is empty. A wet and shining blue Chevy pick-up with a camper attached to the bed is at the kerb. An older black gentleman wearing a straw hat and holding an umbrella is leaning against the truck. Ali walks to the Chevy stiffly, silently, and with great dignity. He has a little trouble getting into his seat on the passenger's side. I close his door. He waves to me.

'Be cool,' he says. I wait for the rest of his catchphrase. But he surprises me once again. 'Remain wise,' he says.

It is 6 February, three weeks after Ali's fiftieth birthday (and my fortieth). A light snow is falling on the village of Berrien Springs, Michigan. It sparkles on Ali's oak-, maple- and birch-lined driveway. My six-year-old son Isaac is with me. He's never met The Champ and I've always wanted him to.

We drive past the small barn where Ali keeps a boxing ring and training bags, pass several other buildings and look down on the St Joseph River, which flows slowly, muddily past Ali's eighty-eight acre farm. We pull up behind the modest white-frame house and park beside the brown-and-beige Rolls-Royce.

Lonnie Ali opens the door to the kitchen. The fourth Mrs Ali grew up in Louisville across the street from the Cassius Clay Sr residence. Like Ali's mom, Lonnie is light-skinned, splashed with a galaxy of freckles, and her hair has an aura of redness to it. Lonnie is a private person, shy and gentle but not gullible, and when she laughs, which is often, she sounds kind. She and Muhammad were married in Louisville in November 1986, shortly after she earned her MBA from UCLA. Lonnie is a thoughtful, guarded speaker, and her reputation in her husband's business affairs is one of shrewd-ness. Like her husband, she has a dead-on way of looking at you.

She is carrying Ali's toddler son, Asaad Amin Ali. Although he was adopted, Asaad's countenance and complexion are basically flawless, like his father's, and his skin is an identical glowing copper colour. Asaad is large for his age. He has been walking since he was six months and Lonnie now tells me he weighs over thirty pounds.

Isaac and I step through the kitchen and into the family room, a large, warmly lit area with thick wheat-coloured carpet, a forty-six-inch TV, a stereo and a couple of over-stuffed couches. To our right, in the far corner, Ali is sitting at a desk, signing pamphlets. He's not wearing a shirt. He's nearly as round as old Buddha himself.

Ali looks at me and nods, almost invisibly, then reaches his arms out to my son, who moves slowly, reverentially, forward. Ali's arms encircle him. 'You'll remember this when you're an old, old man,' Ali says, both to me and to my son. As he places Isaac on his knee, Ali nods toward me again. He wants to be certain I don't feel slighted. 'Happy birthday, Champ,' I say.

Ali finds a shirt, puts it on and turns to Isaac, who is playing with a toy car. 'Stay here,' he says with respectful authority. 'We'll be back.' He waves for me to follow.

We go outside, stepping across the driveway to the garage. The day glows phosphorescently; snow falls in chunks the size of infants' hands. We enter the garage through a side door and climb a set of stairs. He pulls open a door. An otherwise empty space, about the size of a master bedroom, is piled floor to ceiling with boxes and envelopes and packages. 'This is the mail I don't have time to open,' he says.

'How long did it take to get this much?' I ask.

'About six months.'

I grab the two pieces closest to my foot. The top one is covered with brightly coloured stamps. 'From Indonesia,' the world traveller says. I feel a video-cassette inside. The other is a thick letter on onion-skin paper; the return address is in Kansas.

34

'Want you to help me,' he says. 'Feel bad not bein' able to write everybody.'

This is not an overstatement. Nearly every day, when he is home, Ali invests three to four hours in opening letters and writing replies.

'Want to get a 900 number, where people can call and get a message, where I can talk with them. Want you to find out how to do it.'

'If you want, I'll help,' I say. But there's something I want to know. 'Last year, at the twentieth-anniversary dinner of the first Frazier fight, you got up to speak and ended up talking for probably ten minutes. You didn't slur or stammer, your volume was fine, you were funny, your timing was good.' It's true. He was terrific. And I've seen it on several occasions over the past couple years, always when there are no TV cameras on him. 'How do you do that?' I want to know.

He doesn't tell me. I doubt he knows. Instead, he falls into his old pre-fight voice. 'This is Muhammad Ali, the greatest of all times. I did what I set out to do. Whupped Sonny Liston, whupped Joe Frazier, George Foreman, whupped the United States draft board.'

After thirty seconds or so, he stops and rubs his left hand across his face in the way I do when I've just woken from a night's sleep. 'See wh-wh-what you can find out,' he asks. His voice gurgles like the river behind his property.

As we leave the garage, headed for the house, Lonnie and Asaad and Isaac meet us halfway. 'Saadie wanted to go with you, Muhammad,' Lonnie says. She hands the child to her husband and looks at his feet. He's wearing a pair of slick-soled shiny leather uppers. 'Don't you dare drop that baby,' she says. Her tone is wifely, concerned, not patronising. She turns and goes back to the house. With Ali and Asaad in the lead, we trudge around the driveway. Soon, Ali's son decides he wants down. Ali lowers him to the ground, holding his left hand, and tries to get him to walk. Asaad turns to look at Isaac; he intends to play. I ask Isaac to take Asaad's right hand so he'll go with his daddy. My boy does so in a way that replicates Ali's gentleness. I stay a few feet behind, watching the three of them shuffle along at a toddler's pace. For many minutes, Ali, Asaad and Isaac plod back and forth in a chain through the snow. The only sounds are those of wind in the bare branches of trees and of Ali's scuffling feet and, in the distance, of water tumbling over rocks. Just before we go back inside, I reach to brush melting snow from the children's hair and shoulders, and from Ali's.

Isaac and I stay at the farm for two more days. The Great Man plays with my son for hour upon hour, doing magic tricks, telling ghost stories, chasing him around the house, hiding behind furniture, jumping out to tickle him. When he isn't entertaining Isaac or talking with me, he's often asleep and snoring.

As we're leaving for our long drive home, Ali walks us to the car and closes our doors. It's still snowing, but, surprisingly, there is little accumulation. Just enough to make the asphalt slippery. Like Lonnie, I'm concerned that Muhammad might fall. There's a video camera in the back seat. When I'm certain that Ali's balance is OK, I grab it and push the power button.

Ali sees the camera and opens Isaac's door, snatching up my son and holding him at face level. 'This is the next champion,' he says. 'This man will win the crown in 2020. Look at the face. 2020. Just think about it: I will be the manager: I'll be ninety-three. And we will be the greatest of that day, the greatest of that time.'

Ali places my laughing son back in his seat and points at the lens. 'Watch my feet,' he says in his old voice, the one of smoke and dreams, then turns his back and takes about ten shuffling steps. Looking over his left shoulder, he raises his arms perpendicular to his sides. Then, although he sometimes has trouble walking even on dry land, he seems to levitate about three inches off the ground. The winter light is tawny.

'This is Muhammad Ali in Berrien Springs, Michigan,' he says. 'Ain't nobody else like me. Joe Louis, Ray Robinson, they just boxers. I'm the biggest thing that ever happened in sports. I ain't boastin'; it's just the way it is. From Adam until now, I am the greatest in the recorded history of mankind,' he says to the camera, and to the world.

As we pull out of the driveway, Isaac is sitting in the back of the car, staring out the rear window. I ask my son if he is crying. He nods yes. I ask why. 'He's so cool, I didn't think anybody could be that cool. I just wish he wasn't sick.'

I tell him that it's all right. And I honestly believe that it is. Even more than all right, Ali's life has been exactly what it was intended to be. Ali himself believes this and this is why he so seldom seems frustrated by his health. He will occasionally lament about what he could be doing if he were healthy, but most of the time, when asked about his malady, he says, 'God gives people trials. This is my trial. It's His way of keepin' me humble.'

The following week, I go to Isaac's school to talk with his class about our visit to the farm. I ask the first-graders how many of them have heard of Muhammad Ali; all twenty-three raise their hands. After I speak for a few minutes and answer questions, Isaac reads an Ali story he has written. We then play a videotape that includes highlights from The Champ's career, as well as the levitation scene we'd filmed at the farm. At the end of class, everybody, including the girls, leaps around the room, throwing punches at everybody else.

For days thereafter, my son tells me, he reminds his classmates that they have seen a man named Muhammad Ali who can actually fly.

I invested more time writing this story – four years – than I've spent on any other, and I had greater difficulty selling it, although I feel that it's among my best work.

In December 1989, when I left Ali after my breakfast with him at the Mirage Hotel, I took a long walk with my friend Stephen Brunt, a columnist for the Canadian national newspaper, the Globe and Mail. *Both Stephen and I were in Las Vegas, a place neither of us particularly enjoyed, to cover the third 'Sugar' Ray Leonard – Roberto Duran fight. As I excitedly told Stephen what I'd witnessed about Ali, the nearly mythic nature of it, and how cleansing it had felt, he said that I had to write it. I'd already realised that this was true. It had been only three months since my father had died and I felt a need to do some work that was not disposable but that I could regard as* important *in some small way, that would at least* feel *timeless. After the Christmas holidays (grieving over my dad's death, these were among the most trying days of my life: inexplicably, it seemed to me, I went deaf in my right ear at the table over Christmas dinner; two days later, I could hear again), I began trying to sell the idea to American magazines.*

During the time I was pitching my story – which I'd decided to call 'The Zen of Muhammad Ali' – an article was published in Esquire *about the recent death of Harold Conrad, a famous fight publicist and raconteur who physically resembled Salvador Dali. Conrad, who'd been the publicist for several Ali fights, including the first Liston contest, and who sometimes wrote for* Rolling Stone, *had sat beside me at the Leonard – Duran bout at the Mirage, and we had chatted about, among other things, the current Ali. In the* Esquire *tribute to Conrad, the article's writer made a claim, presented as fact, that Ali's health was such that he could no longer travel and could not speak, that he was, effectively, an invalid. The person who wrote the article had no access to Ali, and most likely had never met him, much less had any knowledge of the details of his health. This rumour was indicative of almost everything being 'reported' during that time in the few thin stories I had read about Ali in magazines and newspapers, seen on television and heard on radio. As I* continued to try to sell 'Zen', New York editors told me that my idea wasn't dark or sensational enough; a West Coast editor winced as he said, 'Ali's entirely too painful to read about.' It did no good to tell the editor (again) that I had recently spent hundreds of hours with Ali and that his story wasn't tragic.

Finally, in July 1990, Paul Scanlon, a senior editor at GQ who had been with Jann Wenner at Rolling Stone during that magazine's formative years – and a guy with whom I felt I shared some values, went for both my idea and the 'Zen' title. I worked passionately on the story day in, day out from the morning I received the assignment until late May 1991. When I delivered it to Scanlon, I was very happy with it; it was my best, most original work to date.

I heard back from Paul after roughly a month. He told me that the managing editor had decided to kill the piece. 'It's not hard reporting and that's what Art wants,' Scanlon told me. 'He says we have better ways to spend our money.'

This sort of thing had happened to me before (most recently at Esquire with the story, 'My Dinner with Ali'), and I didn't get discouraged. Over the next year, I sent 'Zen' to more than a dozen magazines. Every editor who read the piece said that he admired the writing; without exception, I was told that there was no audience for an Ali story. 'Ali's not bankable,' said an editor at Playboy.

In June 1992, I heard that a United Kingdom edition of Esquire had recently been launched. I sent 'Zen' through the post to a former New York Esquire editor who had been relocated to London to get the magazine going (the same guy who had rejected 'My Dinner with Ali'). By the time the package made it to London he'd been dismissed from his duties and was supposedly somewhere in France, attending to his wounds. In less than three weeks, I heard back from someone else at the magazine. 'This is brilliant. It's perfect for our readers,' assistant commissioning editor Greg Williams told me. 'You may find an English audience for your work *more quickly than an American one.' I felt honoured – albeit a bit puzzled – to hear this; my stories, after all, are very American in their subjects and tone. But Greg was right: my writing has generally been much better received in Britain than in the US. I've since written other pieces for Greg both at* Esquire *(where 'Zen' was run in the September 1992 issue) and more recently at* Arena, *where he's become editor-in-chief. And my first two books have sold more copies in London than they have in all of America (and maybe more in some of England's smallest towns than in my own home city of more than 300,000 people).*

Throughout autumn and winter 1992, back in the US, I still couldn't scare up serious interest in 'Zen' from any monthly glossy. In the summer of 1993, I decided to try a couple of Sunday newspaper magazine inserts, where I found a considerably different reception. The first two places I sent 'Zen' were the Miami Herald's Tropic *magazine and the* Chicago Tribune Magazine. *The editors at both almost immediately jumped on the story, offering good money. At least as importantly, my writing and I were treated more respectfully than we had ever been at any New York magazine. In the spring of 1994, Tom Shroder at the* Herald *nominated the piece for the 1994 Pulitzer Prize for feature writing, telling me it was rare to do that for a freelance story. In late 1993 and early 1994, I got on the phone and sold 'Zen' as a cover story to more than twenty newspapers around the US (rewriting the piece, tailoring it appropriately, for every editor with whom I worked), as well as in Ireland, Japan, Brazil and Australia. It was a terrific experience; most editors were receptive and flexible, and they did well by the writing. I received hundreds of letters about the story, and the success of 'Zen' inspired me to write my first book,* The Tao of Muhammad Ali.

THE UMPTEENTH LIFE OF
MUHAMMAD ALI

Los Angeles Times and *Louisville Courier-Journal*, 17 January 1992; *Men's Journal*, November-December 1992; *Detroit News*, *Chicago Sun-Times*, *Miami Herald*, *Houston Chronicle*, and New York *Newsday*, 17 January 1997; *GQ*, March 1997; *Candis*, June 1997; *Kicker Sport Magazin* (Germany), August 1997; *Esquire*, May 1998; sparring segment, *Sports Illustrated*, 9 November 1981; *Louisville Courier-Journal*, 21 October 1987; *Arena*, March 1997; a notable sports story, *The Best American Sports Writing 1993*.

I FIRST MET him face to face in July 1975, though I had seen him thousands of times. My walls were covered with newspaper clippings of his victories, my closet floor littered with articles written in the aftermaths of his few defeats.

He was training for a fight with British champion Joe Bugner that was to take place in Kuala Lumpur, Malaysia. I was twenty-three years old, hard-bodied as a hornet, fighting as a junior-lightweight kickboxer out of Winston-Salem, North Carolina.

While pulling on a pair of blood-red Everlast trunks I'd bought for this occasion, I heard him through the dressing room walls, exhorting spectators who'd each paid one dollar to watch him train. 'I will prove to the whole world that I am not only the greatest boxer of all times,' he said, 'I am the greatest martial artist.'

His was the most elemental voice I'd heard; it sounded huge, melodic, eternal. Listening to him made me so nervous that I shook a little and felt that I needed to pee. The old guy standing in front of me, strapping a pair of rich-smelling, red leather gloves on my arms, looked at me and laughed. 'He won't hurt a little white boy like you,' he said.

I no longer thought of myself as 'little' or as a 'white boy'. The old guy was stooped, his face long. 'Naw, he won't hurt you,' he told me again. 'Not too bad anyways.'

After he had finished tying the gloves, and taping down the laces and had left the room, I paced back and forth, staring at reptilian-barked logs in the walls. When I couldn't stand the wait any longer, I walked out the back door and stepped barefoot past boulders placed in a circle around the cabin. On each rock, a name had been painted in bold, red- and blue-trimmed, white block letters. I read the names: Willie Pep and Ray Robinson, Jack Dempsey and Gene Tunney, Rocky Marciano and Archie Moore, Sonny Liston and Joe Frazier. A rounded chunk of brown lichen-covered granite called Joe Louis had been granted the most honoured position, in front of the main entrance to the gym. I listened to a freight train moaning a long way off. I watched the mailman come and go. 'Good luck, son,' he said, chuckling.

I walked around the side of the cabin and climbed the biggest boulder of all, a flat-topped, five-foot high hunk of hard black coal named Jack Johnson. I stood on the rock, gloved hands at my sides. To calm myself and get my lungs started, I shut my eyes and drew four deep slow breaths. I'd never known my body as well as I did then. I could feel oxygen rush all the way to my toes with each breath I took. With closed eyes, I imagined the very power of the cosmos flowing up from the boulder and into my torso.

He's standing in the centre of his ring when I part the ropes and step through. Insect-looking splotches of dried blood dot the porous canvas under my feet. As I stare up at him, he comes into focus and everything else blurs. And I recognise once again that no one else on the planet looks quite like him. His skin is unmarked and is without wrinkles, and he glows in a way that cannot be seen in photographs or on television.

He introduces me to the crowd as a 'great karate master', an accolade I don't merit. Then he opens his mouth steam-shovel-wide, points his gloved left fist at me and in a voice directed to no one in particular, but to the world in general, he shouts, 'You must be a fool to get in the ring with me. When I'm through, you gonna think you been whupped by Bruce Lee.' He looks at me straight and level. 'Are you scared?' he asks. 'Are you scared? – Just think who you're with. How's it feel, knowin' you're in the ring with The Greatest of All Times?'

He turns to the crowd. 'I am the centre of the universe,' he proclaims. I almost believe him.

The bell rings and he dances to my right around the twenty-foot square of taut canvas. Suddenly I'm no longer nervous. My thighs are strong and springy, there's looseness in my movement.

He bounces from side to side; I feel every step he takes shoot into my feet and up my legs. I bend to the right, toss a jab toward his belt line, straighten, snap a long tentative front-kick to his head. I guess it's the first kick he's had thrown at him, but he pulls away as easily as if he's been dodging feet his entire life. He stops dancing and stands flat-footed in front of me, studying my movements. I try to lever in a jab from the outside. His eyes are snappingly bright. His face is beaming and round and open. He waits until my punch is a half-inch from his nose and pulls his head straight back. I punch nothing but air and dreams. He turns square toward me, teases by sticking out a long white-coated tongue, steps back to the ropes, takes a seat on the second strand where his head is only a little higher than mine, and beckons me in with a brisk wave of gloves.

I block out spectators' laughs and slide inside his arms three half-steps; he's so close I feel his breath on my shoulder. I dig a roundkick into his right kidney, feel his flesh conform to the shape of my shin, see the opening I'm hoping for, fake a jab and explode from my crouch, rocketing a spinning backfist, jab, left-hook combination straight into the centre of the right side of his jaw. The punches feel so good that I smile. People in the crowd *ooh* and *aah*.

He opens his eyes fried-egg-wide in feigned disbelief. He has never thought of me before, will never think of me as a fighter again, but for two seconds I deserve his serious attention. For two long seconds we are inseparably bound, whirling in a galaxy of electricity, each seeing nothing but the other. For two week-long seconds I am flying. Then he comes off the ropes and squashes me with one flyswatter jab.

I see the punch coming; it's a piece of hot red candy exactly the size of a gloved fist. I try to slip to the side and can't – it's that fast. The back of my head bounces off my shoulders. A chorus of white light goes off behind my eyes. There's a metal taste in my mouth, then a second heavier thump as he catches me with a left hook I don't see. The spectators sound way, way off; my legs go to soup beneath me.

He knows I'm hurt and he steps back. Then his eyes go kind, he slides an arm around my shoulders, we exchange hugs and smiles, and it's over.

But I've accomplished something I'd never, yet always, believed I'd have opportunity to do.

I have boxed with Muhammad Ali.

As we leave the ring together, my childhood idol and the greatest of all pugilists speaks in a way few men have ever talked to me – softly, gently, almost purring. 'You're not as dumb as you look,' he says. 'You're fast. And you sure can hit to be *sssooo* little.'

He may as well have said he was adopting me.

I begin to quake. My insides dance. But I manage to stay composed long enough to say the one thing I hope will (and

44

which seems to) impress him most. With confidence I've learned from watching him on television and hearing him on the radio countless times, I say simply, 'I know.'

I first became a serious Ali watcher in January 1964, an obsession that stayed with me throughout my teen years. While at university, my first story for a major national magazine was about a seminal Ali experience – my 1975 sparring session with him, when, because of his influence, I was hoping to become a world champ myself. In September 1977, my girlfriend Lyn and I eloped and unsuccessfully tried to get married at the Ali–Earnie Shavers bout. By 1986, when I became the district manager of a video store chain in Ali's hometown of Louisville, Kentucky, I seldom thought about him.

My first day in Louisville, driving to one of my shops with the company president, he pointed across the street and said, 'Muhammad Ali's mom lives there.' From then on, my eyes were riveted on the house whenever I passed by. On the Friday before Easter 1989, a block-long white Winnebago was parked out front.

I worked up courage, went to the door of the Winnebago, knocked. Ali opened the door, looking as big as God. He leaned under the frame to see me, waved me in, did magic tricks, invited me to stay for dinner.

For several years after that, I saw a lot of Ali. I've written stories about him and our relationship, as well as my first book, *The Tao of Muhammad Ali*, a non-fiction novel about the ways he has influenced my life. Because of Ali, I have found my voice: I am now a writer.

One thing I purposely didn't do in *The Tao of Muhammad Ali*, but which I hope to accomplish with this article, is to provide a current Ali report card. Like almost everyone who was born before 1970, I can't help but remember a time when Ali seemed to be constantly moving inside a private and wondrous rhythm, when his eyes shone like electric black-berries, when heat shimmered from his almost perfectly symmetrical torso. The young Ali's seemingly endless energy promised that he would never get old. Now, in many ways, he's older than just about anyone his age.

Yet, when you know Ali personally, you don't feel bad for him. He is not the first artist to have suffered for, or because of, his beliefs. Though his ego is no smaller than it once was, in many ways Ali is relieved that it's been a long while since he's felt the need to play the role of Allah's angry avatar. 'I see those old fights and interviews,' he says, 'and I can't believe that's me.' Ali today is among the happiest people I've known; many of his day-to-day activities have a quality about them that might best be described as soberly magical.

Ali always calls me 'my man'. Although I've spent days and days with him, he never remembers my name. This is not indicative of serious mind-fry (he would've done the same when he was young and healthy). It's more a product of having met probably half the people on the planet. Maybe most important, though, it seems related to a choice he made decades ago not to get weighed down with names and other basically insignificant details.

Ali often speaks in a halting voice that sounds as thin as tissue paper and issues from high in his throat. When sitting, he drifts in and out of sleep. At night, he often wakes; he seldom gets as much rest as he needs. These patterns do not mean that he is listless. Contrary to popular perception, he has an amazingly high energy level and is gifted with enormous stamina. Every year I have known him, he has travelled the globe for many weeks in a row, making appearances and being on the move for up to eighteen hours a day.

There are nearly constant tremors in his hands, particularly the left, and when he is concentrating or anxious (as when he feels compelled to perform in front of television cameras), his head shakes, more so when he is tired. His facial features have the muscular rigidity – the 'mask' – that is associated with Parkinsonism. He is more expressive with friends and with children. His eyes are inordinately sensitive to light; for this reason, he often wears sunglasses. When in a bright room or in direct sunlight, he blinks rapidly. In the hundreds and hundreds of hours I've spent with him, only twice have I seen him frustrated by his health. 'God gives people trials,' he says. 'This is my trial. It's His way of keepin' me humble.'

He also has regular coughing, wheezing bouts with bronchitis, which people often misassociate with his Parkinson's syndrome. And he rarely does what's best for his health. Although he hasn't eaten pork since 1963 (it is forbidden by Muslim dietary codes), he doesn't usually refuse much of anything else, and he has a serious penchant for desserts, particularly vanilla ice cream, of which he'll eat as much as half a gallon a day.

His symptoms become more pronounced when he has travelled through numerous time zones and when he has been away from home for many days. 'Muhammad's problem is he won't take his medicines,' says his wife, Lonnie. 'You know Muhammad – he's been home now for a week and he hasn't taken them more than once.'

Ali regularly sits on the edge of conversations, listening. With his children, wife and friends, much communication is non-verbal; the art of the gesture has become quite important for Ali. When he talks, he usually chooses his words with precision. Asked why, unlike the old days, everyone everywhere seems to love him, he spreads the fingers of his trembling left hand and says, 'It's because of this. I'm more human now.'

People everywhere are concerned not only about Ali's health, but about his ability to support himself. They needn't worry: financially, he's comfortable; he makes more than a million dollars every year.

His principal source of income is derived from trust funds.

He owns an eighty-eight-acre estate and almost modest house in Berrien Springs, Michigan, though he and Lonnie perpetually say they are shopping for a home and property in Louisville. Ali also owns his old Deer Lake training camp in Pennsylvania and much of the mountain on which it was built, as well as several automobiles, including a Rolls-Royce.

Lonnie Ali grew up in Louisville across the street from the Cassius Clay Sr residence. She has known Ali since she was five years old and he was nineteen. By the time she was six, she said that she would marry him. Her mother, Marguerite Williams, was Mrs Clay's best friend. She and Muhammad were married in Louisville in 1986, after he supported her while she earned her MBA from UCLA.

The family member closest to Ali was his mother, who died in August 1994. Ali went into a period of depression after Mrs Clay's death, during which his Parkinsonism seemed to worsen. My kids and I hung out with him for several days that October in Baltimore and again that November in Louisville. As he moved from appearance to appearance, signing autographs, he looked removed, as if from another dimension, and there'd often be globules of drool on his bottom lip. As he felt them, he'd subtly bend his head, tug at the left lapel of his suit jacket, and discreetly wipe the spittle above the inside breast pocket. The label on Ali's suit pocket read 'THE GREATEST' in red stitching designed to resemble Arabic letters.

After his appearance at the 1996 Olympics and millions of people's renewed interest in him, Ali's physical condition improved a little. For more than a decade, when he's been home, he invests two to four hours each day in signing Muslim handouts and photos of himself, replying to fan mail (he receives thousands of letters each month), reading the Koran and praying. He also regularly accepts visitors, particularly if they have children.

Children, anybody's children, remain one of Ali's great pleasures. 'When I was thirty,' he confides, 'I used to wonder when I was gowna quit playin' with kids. Used to sorta worry about it. Now, I know I'm never gowna quit.'

Ali has six children from previous marriages, as well as two from mothers he did not marry, but whom he supports. His ninth and youngest is Asaad, an adopted boy whose peach-core-coloured skin glows like his father's.

Ali doesn't see much of the people who were with him during his ring career. Street mystic and raconteur Drew 'Bundini' Brown died in 1988. Ali's father, Cassius Marcellus Clay Sr, died in February 1990. Ali runs into trainer Angelo Dundee three or four times a year. 'We're as close as we've ever been,' Dundee says. 'But he's busy doing one thing, I'm busy with my thing.' The member of his former entourage he sees most often is his photographer and best friend, Howard Bingham, who often travels with Ali and talks with him on the phone nearly every day.

Ali is unquestionably the most generous person I've known. This munificence has allowed him to be taken for tens of millions of dollars, often by those he has called his friends.

One of the more remarkable abusers is an attorney named Arthur Morrison who helped arrange Ali's 1990 visit to wartime Baghdad. Unbeknown to Ali, who saw his trip to Iraq as a peace mission, Morrison tried to make a few Eurodollars for himself by transporting a boxing ring to an area near Saudi Arabia's border with Kuwait and coercing our ailing legend into fighting a ten-round exhibition. He was unsuccessful in his effort and is no longer associated with Ali.

Does Ali know that he has been taken advantage of? Does he mind? 'I want to do as much as I can for everybody who deserves it,' he says.

The Tao of Muhammad Ali has become something of a phenomenon in England, Scotland, Ireland, Japan and Australia, but has gotten scant attention in the U.S. I've urged myself towards finding an Ali-esque pleasure in this. As I struggle to pay weekly bills, I'm reminded that the guy who calls me 'my man' was regarded as a citizen of the world – and particularly of Britain – years before his own countrymen came to appreciate him.

I'm often asked why I named the book, *The Tao of Muhammad Ali*. Two reasons worth mentioning: first, the Chinese word Tao translates as way. When I was growing up in the sixties and seventies, I thought of myself as following in the way of Muhammad Ali. In addition, over the years, I've come to regard Ali as sort of a subconscious Taoist; there is no way to accurately define who he is, no way to categorise him. There is something liberating about this, as there is to the time I've spent with him. Being around Ali has always emptied me, opened me up, freed me. He allows me to feel genuinely childlike, almost entirely unboxed. And he seems to have this effect on a whole bunch of folks.

In August 1996, as Ali stood at the top of a stadium in Atlanta, his left hand dramatically shaking as he held the torch with which he would light the Olympic flame, many people came to recognise what I've known about The Champ for a very long time – his current story is not tragic; indeed, there's a kind of beauty to it.

A positive thing about Ali's Parkinson's syndrome is that it has allowed him to become an ailing family member to the world. To some of us he is father or grandfather; to others, he is uncle, cousin, brother, nephew. As has been the case for so many of the identities Ali has worn, I know of no one else for whom this mythology has been true. As Ali long ago reinvented not only boxing but many of our ideas of celebrity, he is now reinventing our notions of personal illness. His own weighty yet gentle myth has become this: No one, not even The Greatest of All Times, can defy gravity.

Appropriately, Ali's American Express card reads 'G.O.A.T. [Greatest of All Times], *Inc.*'

'I ain't nothin but an old goat,' he explains. 'It's the God in people that connects them to me.'

The sparring scene at the beginning of this piece was first published entirely on its own. I wrote it in 1979 and 1980 while I was a student at East Carolina University in Greenville, North Carolina. My writing instructor, the novelist Terry Davis, suggested that I send it to Sports Illustrated. *They bought it and ran it the following year, when Ali was training to fight Trevor Berbick in what would become his last professional contest. The $750 I was paid was a lot of money to me. I bought a used video-cassette recorder, a VHS tape called* Muhammad Ali's Greatest Fights *and a copy of* Enter the Dragon. *It was the first time I had been published (and I'd not sell a story again for nearly eight years). I ordered thirty copies of the magazine from the neighbourhood newsagent and when they arrived, sent one to everyone I knew. In its original form, the story was intended to be the opening chapter of a book that over the next two decades would develop into two volumes,* The Tao of Muhammad Ali *and* The Tao of Bruce Lee.

THE YIN AND THE YANG OF
MUHAMMAD ALI

SEPTEMBER 1992. MUHAMMAD Ali has just returned home from South Bend, where his friend Howard Bingham drove him to get his hair dyed and sculpted for the pictures we'll be taking. The photographer I've brought from *Rolling Stone* is outside setting up his first portrait and Ali and I are sitting on straight-backed chairs near his downstairs desk, a three-foot-deep by four-foot-high collapsing old corrugated box between us. As always at Ali's house, the wall-sized television behind us is wailing. Weathercasters are warning of a late-summer stormfront that's stampeding across the plains and Lake Michigan from the west. The front will arrive this afternoon, accompanied by dramatic hail, sustained seventy-five-mile-an-hour winds and tornadoes of such size and fury that even Pecos Bill couldn't have lassoed and ridden them.

Ali's paying no attention to the television. To him, the weather is seemingly of little consequence. His gaze is religiously fixed on the container between us. As we sit in our chairs, he tugs them one by one from elbow-deep in the box – some in colour, many in black and white, some faded to pinks and greys and teal, others dramatically bent and creased, many of them Howard's photos, some simple snapshots, others eight-by-ten artist's proofs, few ever published; some taken thirty years before, others within the past several months, all of them collected randomly in this rag-tag over-sized container. Photos of Ali with Martin Luther King,

Malcolm X, Jimmy Carter, Gerald Ford, Rosa Parks, Johnny Cash, JohnPaulGeorgeRingo, Elvis; with Johnny Carson, Ella Fitzgerald, Diana Ross, Marvin Gaye, Sam Cooke, 'Little' Stevie Wonder; with Ray Robinson, Joe Louis – and with a solar system of other world champion boxers, most of whom are paying homage to The Greatest of them all; with Madonna, Bill Clinton, Nelson Mandela, his mother, his father, his wives and children. Thousands upon thousands of photographs.

He painstakingly, meticulously extracts each from the top of the box, talismanically holds it up for me to acknowledge. Points and stares at me to confirm that I understand its place in his own theology before dropping it on a short stack on the floor to his left and moving to the next magic image. Slowly, he lifts a relatively recent snapshot of a copper-skinned infant in a pink dress lying in a baby carrier, stares at it five seconds, then, without purposely showing the photo to me, he stands with the picture between thumb and forefinger. He trudges away, tugs the wastebasket from beside his desk, methodically brings it to his chair, sits beside me again – and very carefully tears the snapshot once, twice, three times with shaking fingers, and drops the pieces in the garbage bin before going back to the corrugated box to consider another image.

Every moment I have spent with Muhammad Ali has had its own particular resonance, its own weather. I'll not tell you what I believe the story I've just shared reveals; I'll let you decide for yourself.

I will, however, say this: people all around the world admire Ali, not only for the obvious reasons – the singular grace with which he fought for almost twenty-five years; his boastful, glowing prettiness; his huge charm and presence; his contagious and distinctive humour; his brave stand against the Vietnam War; the great dignity with which he carried himself through his afflicted middle years – but also because for five decades, no matter what outrageousness has leaped from his limbs and his mouth, and regardless of how extensively he has been marketed and self-marketed, we recognise that Ali has always shown us something also intensely human, ringingly true. And we well understand how uncommon this level of honesty is among public personalities. Apparently, however, fewer and fewer of us (Joe Frazier being the obvious exception) realise that, although Ali is in some ways one of the most 'real' people we're ever likely to see, there are ways that this felt-in-our-bellies honesty is chimeric.

Since his trembling appearance at the 1996 Olympics, it has become fashionable to regard Ali as a stricken, mute saint. That notion differs greatly from Muhammad Ali, the actual human being. The Muhammad Ali I have spent hundreds and hundreds of hours with is both meditative and manic, inane and insightful, observant and distracted, monastically quiet and riot-noisy, amazingly gentle and occasionally scary, surprisingly brilliant and basically retarded, very well-balanced and, it often seems, genuinely nuts.

Within the past decade, in a boxing gym, I have watched him let rage course through his body, flow down his arms and out through his fists as he boxed a college kid silly simply because the boy was big enough to look like he could take an Ali whupping – and because it felt good to Ali to trash the kid. I have sat with him at his mother's house and listened to him mourn his sex life with a former wife. '*Maaann*, she's a fox,' he told me. 'Yeah, Champ,' I said, 'but you got a good wife now. And a good life.' He looked at me very intently. 'Man, but Veronica, she's a *fox,*' he said with such profundity you'd believe he'd discovered a huge planet circling the sun. I have watched him hold a documentary film crew hostage (with whom he had a contract to shoot a multimillion-dollar feature) until the director gave him several hundred dollars in pocket cash so that Ali would begin that day's filming. I have seen him hand out dozens and dozens of hundred-dollar bills to destitute strangers on rough street corners. I have had him lean toward me to say, 'I'm gowna be remembered as a prophet. I've brought more people to my religion than anybody else in history.' I have stared as he exploded at Muslim associates for taking advantage of him: 'It's my belt,' he roared in his Philadelphia hotel room after the 1991 dinner celebrating the twentieth anniversary of the first Frazier fight, gently pushing me out of the way and stepping around Jim Brown to recover a heavyweight championship belt presented to him that evening by World Boxing Association president Bob Lee – a belt to replace the ones that Ali had lost, had gotten stolen and that he'd given away – and that Muslim handlers were ostensibly trying to protect by keeping it from him. 'Give me my muthafuckin belt,' he shouted, soot and smoke and choler in his voice, yanking it from the fingers of a short, heavy, middle-aged woman and deeding it immediately and for ever more to his daughter Maryum. And I have been riding with him in the back of a black rented limousine when he turned to me and without any prompting said, 'Imagine what I could be *doin'*, if I didn't have this shit,' meaning his Parkinsonism.

Why do I show you these basically private moments that Ali himself will surely be upset I've revealed? 'I am human, and nothing human is foreign to me,' the Roman dramatist Terence wrote roughly one hundred years before the birth of Jesus. I can't think of a more mature, truthful, affirming statement about what it means to be a person, any person, every person. And there is much that I feel Muhammad Ali and the people closest to him, particularly his wife Lonnie, can learn from Terence.

August 1996. The month before, I'd sent Muhammad and Lonnie several copies of the proofs of my first book, *The Tao of Muhammad Ali*. Nervous and anxious but excited to get their reactions, I call their number. Lonnie answers the phone. When she recognises my voice, I feel her go cold; the phone suddenly gets heavier in my hand. This is not a situation I've had with her before. I ask what's wrong.

'The things you said in that book,' she tells me. 'The things about Muhammad that weren't true.'

'Weren't true? What did I say that isn't true?'

'You wrote about him with a hole in his T-shirt,' she says, her voice weighted, mechanical, on guard.

'What?'

'You said you saw him with a hole in his shirt,' says Ali's wife. 'I'd never let him go out of the house like that.'

'Aw, Lonnie, come on – you've got to be kidding. You're mad at me for what? – because I write about him having a hole in a T-shirt. Well, what can I say . . . it was there. That's not demeaning to Ali. It humanises him. It helps folks relate to him as one of us.'

Lonnie hesitates before answering. 'Look, Davy, I have to go,' she finally tells me. 'I don't have time for this now. Maybe we can talk later.'

But we didn't. And over the years since that phone call, I've had almost no contact with Ali or Lonnie. I don't believe it's an overstatement to say that they've avoided me. And during the time that I've not seen the Alis, I believe I've come to understand that Lonnie's problem with me is more fundamental than either what she said, or was able to name. It has a lot to do with demythologising Ali; to demythologise is not exactly Lonnie's goal.

Throughout the 1990s and into the early twenty-first century, as Ali has approached his sixtieth year, and as the symptoms of his Parkinsonism have become ever more prominent, he has been inordinately obsessed with his mortality; indeed, Ali carries the aura of his own impermanence with him in every moment. During this same period, from what I can see and have heard, Ali, Lonnie and Howard Bingham, who has been Ali's best friend since the mid-1960s, have laboured daily to perpetuate the polished and shining image that Ali wishes to leave as a legacy – what might be called the historical Ali. One of the tactics they've used to aid in the creation of this narrative is to repress those things that could possibly be regarded as unseemly. This 'official' Ali can be paralleled to the ever-growing rigour of his Parkinsonism, as if with each step he takes he becomes more a creation – a living statue – and less the irrepressible character so many of us have adored (and many have reviled) for all these decades. The effect is this: guarding his pyramid, Ali is becoming his very own sandstone Sphinx.

Those of us who write as part of our way of life can understand, and sympathise with, the Ali family's ache for respectful perpetuity. It is, after all, one of the major (although deluded) reasons that just about all writers write and maybe all artists perform art. And it is, of course, the chief reason that religions exist: our species seems to have a desperate, perhaps biological, need to seek our own immortality.

Toward that end – and I suppose to increase their personal income, having trademarked Ali's name and likeness – over the past several years, the Ali family have shut down fans' Internet sites and prevented films that they have found displeasing from being released on home video. Their primary means of accomplishing this has been by suing, and/or threatening to sue. While online recently, I found the following note on the single page of what had been a multi-page fansite: 'I had this site of pictures of my hero, Muhammad Ali. I don't make money from it and I haven't tried to. But I've been getting letters from Ali's lawyers telling me I have to shut down or they're going to sue me. This makes me very sad. Ali is not my hero anymore.' In addition, Ali's attorneys have recently sued a fan who attended the 1974 Ali–Foreman bout and regularly displayed photos he shot of the fight in his art gallery in Los Angeles.

The obvious irony is this: Muhammad Ali, the little guy bullied and oppressed in the 1960s by the big bad system (including boxing commissions and the United States government) has now become the bully. 'I don't know many saints who employ a platoon of lawyers,' says George Tanakos, a film producer and distributor who, in 1999, released video cassettes of Ali's 1976 'martial arts' match with professional wrestler Antonio 'the Pelican' Inoki, during which Inoki crawled crab-style around the ring on his back for almost the entire fifteen rounds, kicking at Ali's shins and knees while Ali looked embarrassed and threw a total of seven punches in the entire 'contest'. In March 2000, Ali and his attorneys filed suit against Tanakos and Xenon Entertainment to remove their Ali cassette from stores, saying that their programme 'has irreparably harmed and will continue to irreparably harm Mr Ali's reputation'. Tanakos and the president of Xenon complied with Ali's request. 'If he came to the courtroom," explains Tanakos, 'with the way he looks and moves – not to mention how much everybody cares about him, we would not have had a chance.' Even though the Inoki tape was no longer available, that wasn't enough to satisfy Ali's attorneys. Tanakos and Xenon had sold less than two thousand copies of their programme and had lost money on the title. Yet to avoid a jury trial, Ali's attorneys required Tanakos to pay a sizeable cash settlement to Ali.

Regarding Ali's image, such legal orchestration is hardly necessary: his legacy is as assured as anyone's can be. Muhammad Ali is more famous, and more admired, than virtually anyone else has been, ever, in his own lifetime. And as is true of the fable that American schoolchildren are taught about George Washington chopping down his father's cherry tree and not being capable of lying about it, these efforts by Ali and his family and attorneys to 'refine' his personal history serve not only to narrow and devalue that narrative (as well as his humanity) – but our own. Denying the full range of his humanity, who is Ali wanting to impress? Allah? Or maybe Ali feels he needs to deceive himself.

An implicit motivator in this self-serving history-sculpting is the keep-the-slaves-in-their-places Judaeo/Christian/Islamic idea that it is somehow 'bad' and 'wrong' to be who we are, to be simply human – and I feel that this regressive puritanism has contributed greatly to Lonnie Ali's problems with my writing, and therefore with me.

In traditional Asian cultures, there is no good and evil; there is simply that which *is*. That view of the world is not reductionist or relativist; indeed, because of the bone-deep ways we've been propagandised by our tough old Man on His mountaintop religions, it's an understanding that Westerners have difficulty growing into. The Asian (non) concept is this: it's an attempt to come nakedly to this life, to recognise the world as it exists — and to accept it.

The untameable Muhammad Ali that hundreds of millions of us care most about has the option and the ability to decide not to live the age-old boogieman lie about our own intrinsic human evil. 'I don't have to be who you want me to be,' Ali said way back in 1964. The older Ali doesn't have to play the role of good slave accepting the propaganda of the 'Good' Book. One of the most important things I've learned from Ali is that human beings – living, breathing, hurting, weeping, screaming, laughing, dreaming, shining *people* – are considerably more interesting, and *real*, than saints or other shadow-and-mist icons. It is a lesson that Ali himself may not know he was teaching – but one that would well serve my childhood idol, mentor and friend to notice, remember and appreciate.

PART TWO: ZEN FISTICUFFS

Rapture

Sport, July 1989.

MY DAUGHTER IS seven years old. Her name is Johanna. Johanna doesn't like prizefights or prizefighters. I don't often watch fights around Johanna, but when I do she calls them dumb. The day before yesterday I returned home from interviewing Thomas Hearns and Ray Leonard in Atlanta. Johanna knew before I left that I would be interviewing two prizefighters. She didn't know who they were and had not seen either man compete – but she knew that they were dumb. The night I got home from my interviews, the Ray Leonard – Marvin Hagler fight was being replayed on ESPN. Johanna was sitting beside me when I stumbled across the bout while flipping channels. 'That's Sugar Ray Leonard,' I told her. 'He's the one I interviewed in Atlanta.'

'Which one is he?' she wanted to know.

'The one with tassels on his shoes,' I said.

She did not call Ray Leonard dumb. She watched two complete rounds and then announced, 'I like Sugar Ray Leonard. I want to see the whole fight.'

The CNN control booth was crowded. An attractive young camera operator was counting heads: 'twenty-five, twenty-six, twenty-seven – most people we've ever had in here –

twenty-eight, twenty-nine, thirty, thirty-one. Is everybody on his payroll?'

The 'his' she was referring to was Sugar Ray Leonard, who had just completed an interview and was sitting behind the desk where it had taken place, leaning comfortably forward in a swivel chair, his neck and shoulders entirely relaxed, with his nose pressed hard and flat against that of Thomas 'the Hit Man' Hearns.

'No,' I said, 'most of them are on *his* payroll.' My 'his' was boxing promoter Bob Arum, who was seated on a grey-carpeted platform at the opposite end of the room from Leonard and Hearns, and who was carefully watching a replay of the interview. I walked across the room to Arum, introduced myself, and asked the very question I was sure he'd heard a thousand times since the two boxers had signed contracts to meet for a second time on 12 June 1989.

'No way these guys are fighting just for the money,' was Arum's immediate reply. 'I'll tell you right now, this is the easiest big fight I ever made. It took only ten days. That just doesn't happen. Money was not an issue. I told both parties what we could do and they took it.'

I wanted to know Arum's opinion of why Hearns and Leonard were fighting one another. 'Different reasons,' he said. 'Tommy's doing it for revenge. He thinks Ray's cheated him out of the recognition he deserves, out of his proper place in history. And Ray – Sugar Ray Leonard is fighting to take advantage of his art, of his skills in the ring.'

Arum and company are billing this bout as 'The War'. It is, of course, late twentieth-century hype at its crassest. But make no mistake: though the 1989 version of Hearns is rumoured to be only a few solid punches away from retirement, there's volatile chemistry between these fellows. The night of 12 June won't be easy for either contestant.

In the legendary first fight in 1981, Hearns's chin and legs were exposed to be less than perfect. Leonard suffered an injury to his left eye that would lead to a detached retina.

Images from that contest have resonance. Consider the best-known photograph – Sugar Ray's eye swollen nearly closed, his gloved fists thrust godlike above his head, his back to Hearns, whose long thin body sags among the ropes, looking for all the world like a broken spider's. Recall that same spindliness, the terrible and beautiful mortality, as Hearns was carried from the ring following his third-round knockout loss to Marvellous Marvin Hagler. Now think about this – those bouts took place nearly a decade ago.

And, these eight and a half years later, both Leonard and Hearns are risking humiliation and a soured reputation, not to mention health.

It is, of course, entirely possible that both older warriors will transcend the apparent limitations of their bodies and give us a drama comparable to the epic third Ali–Frazier bout – the Thrilla in Manila – in which both men fought hard and gloriously, well past their primes, in what has since become regarded as one of the best (and, unfortunately, most brutal) fights in boxing history.

But neither Ali nor Frazier were ever again complete athletes (or undamaged men) after that night. Hearns and Leonard might not be after 12 June. Again – why take the chance? Money?

Hearns gave his answer on the ride back to the hotel. He was sitting in the centre of the black leather rear seat, dressed in a black pinstripe Mafioso-style suit and shiny black shoes. Both of his hands were open, palms down on his knees, and he seldom shifted to the left or the right or changed expressions. Thomas Hearns is not known for speaking easily to interviewers. His silence says he chooses space, needs space and knows how to get it.

'I've thought about him every day and night for eight years,' Hearns said, speaking of Leonard and corroborating Arum's hyperbole. 'I need to get rid of him. I need to think clearly. He's standing in my way from being remembered as one of the greatest boxers ever.

'The only time I don't think about him is when I'm fighting somebody else. Boxing makes me happy, I'm a happy fighter. There's nobody to blame or nobody to support you. And nobody to take credit for what you do. You stand alone out there under the lights. I like the lights shining on me. I like the way it feels. I'm more awake, more alive when I'm fighting.'

Hearns says he places little value on talk, but he speaks like he fights, with precision, economy and power.

We shook hands, Sugar Ray Leonard and I. His hand was small, the skin baby smooth. As is true of every boxer I've met, the handshake was gentle, even girlish.

We were in his room on the twenty-seventh floor of the Hilton. He was dressed in a custom-tailored, banded-collar, blue pinstriped shirt, a burgundy cashmere jacket, black custom-tailored trousers with form-fitting elastic cuffs and a pair of black Mandarin slippers. It was 9.25 a.m. He was standing at the window, looking out across the skyline as if it were he, not Ted Turner, who owned this city of Atlanta.

'My perceptions are better when I'm training,' he said, without being asked. 'Sometimes people don't believe me, or they think it sounds funny, but I'm more aware of things going on around me, and I miss that when I'm not training.'

He asked me to take a seat with him at a glass coffee table. There were black tea bags, cups and a pot of hot water. His hands did not look out of place when he wrapped them around the small, fragile cup.

I asked, 'At this point in your career, what is the most important reason you're fighting?'

'For the love,' he said. 'There are very, very few people who can do what I do. I think people misunderstand my reasons for fighting. I'm enjoying and taking advantage of my skills while I've got them.'

And what skills those have been! Even in lesser performances, Leonard has moved with grace and finesse. And if finesse isn't beautiful, and if beauty isn't among the qualities intrinsic to art, then I have never met an artist.

It is important to fistic artists such as Leonard to do what they do with beauty. Although it may appear that the best of boxers move effortlessly, it is much more difficult to fight with beauty and with science than without. When you see a fighter attempting to move gracefully, you can be certain that fellow has made a commitment to be an artist of the ring. He wouldn't fight without being paid to do so, and he certainly hopes to make a mansion full of money, but the dollars are not enough for this bloke.

'There is nothing to compare to being at the top of your industry, to stand out on top with everybody else taking potshots,' Leonard continued. 'It's enormously gratifying. I don't know how long it'll last, but it doesn't matter. What matters is it's now, *right now*. It's happening.'

I'd heard this before from boxers: the importance of feeling you're living in the now, in the moment, at the centre of everything around you. There is an immediacy of life unique to the athlete.

'I believe in predestination,' Leonard said. 'This stuff is meant to happen. Even when I was a kid, I had a huge imagination. I always found myself flying, at night in dreams and then when I'd be walking down the street imagining it, you know, being special, being an exception. Boxing lets me continue to do that. It brings out the kid in me and lets me make a living by being a kid. There's no greater feeling than to work out, especially when you're *there*. It's exhilarating to be in the ring, moving around. Your body's in tune, it's toned, your reactions are quick, your mind's quick, you feel absolutely immortal.

'You want immortality. Even if you don't know it, you want it. You want this to continue for the rest of your life, and you never want your life to end. Sometimes I think, "I don't want to die, man, I'm not finished yet." Life is so, so . . . delicate. I hate to watch television – kids dying, old people shot here, shot there. And I'm saying, "Hey, I want to keep doing this," because I never think about history, but down deep I'm doing it for history, to leave a legacy.'

Leonard uses words less sparingly than Hearns, but in intention and in substance, what each man had to say was scarcely different from the other. Both boxers seem to be fighting for similar basic reasons. Chief among these is a nearly mystical phenomenon that might be called the rapture of the ring.

I've known dozens of good boxers. All of them talk among themselves about feeling more alive when fighting than at other times in their lives. What they mean is that they work in accelerated fields of concentration, in worlds of heightened detail and awareness, that most of us never know. When they are fighting well, movement is relaxed and in the flow: the mind is clean and they move *inside* rhythm. A time distortion occurs. Seconds feel like minutes, minutes seem like hours. All detail becomes important. The rest of existence seems less real than what is being experienced in the lighted ring. And it is the pursuit (and memory – memory not of the mind but of the body) of this rapture of the ring, more than money, that is the reason older champions keep making unfortunate comebacks.

There are good champions and there are great champions. Ray Leonard and Thomas Hearns have both striven to be among the best of champions. Boxers at this level have yet another reason for fighting – a need to feel they are doing something of lasting importance, something that will secure for them a place in history. I doubt these are usually conscious desires; they're more a biological groping, a manifestation of our species' innate desire for continuance.

I recall a television documentary in honour of Aaron Copland on his eighty-fifth birthday. The composer of *Appalachian Spring* and *Billy the Kid* told an interviewer, 'There's no greater reward than having been able to make my living creating something that will outlive me.' Most of us look for immortality in religion, through our children, in possessions we collect, in names we give fellowships and buildings, on our tombstones, through our work. Boxing champions look for immortality in four-cornered rings.

And so it is that on the night of 12 June 1989, Thomas Hearns and Ray Charles Leonard will again climb through the ropes to pursue that great singular piece of work. This afternoon I bought a video cassette of the Leonard–Marvin Hagler fight for my daughter Johanna, who certainly does not consider any boxing match to be art and who, having had a fortunate seven years, knows little of her own mortality. Yet, when watching the Hagler bout, Johanna reacted instinctively to the beauty with which Sugar Ray Leonard moves, and despite my ambivalence about romanticising a business fuelled by blood, I intend to ask Leonard to sign the videotape for Johanna in the hope that she might some day share it (and this story) with her children.

This pre-fight article marked the first time a magazine editor called me and offered a writing assignment, and the second Leonard–Hearns contest was the first time I had sat ringside at a major boxing match. Although most ringside talk among boxing insiders was that Hearns would be quickly disposed of, I was certain that it would be a long night for both contestants. It was: the fight was a twelve-round, relentlessly hard-fought draw. In almost 100-degree heat and stark desert light, Leonard was knocked down in rounds three and eleven; he boxed Hearns all over the ring in the fifth and particularly in the final round; both men were hurt on several occasions, both finished the contest bloodied and swollen, on their feet, unbowed. At the end of the fight Hearns was buoyant: he said he had been delivered from a weight he'd been forced to endure since the first bout. For the next couple of years, as the boxing editor and writer for Sport *magazine (I was offered that role partly because of this piece), when I interviewed Tommy for stories and saw him both at his home and at boxing events, he smiled easily and often and talked freely and openly. It was a pleasure to spend time with him.*

WANTING TO WHUP SUGAR RAY

Washington Post Magazine, 3 February 1991; *Sport*, March 1991; a notable sports story, *The Best American Sports Writing 1992*.

IN THE FALL of 1979, I was attending East Carolina University in Greenville, North Carolina. In addition to taking fiction and non-fiction writing classes and obsessively working to learn to write, I taught self-defence two nights a week and was pretending to myself that I might become the world's greatest martial artist.

When I switched on the television in those days, I almost never turned to boxing. I believed that the only boxer from whom there was something to learn was Muhammad Ali. Ali had recently retired, and my youthful opinion was that there was no one else worth studying.

In late November, eastern North Carolina received its largest snowfall on record. The town of Greenville, where it typically snows no more than once every ten years, didn't have equipment to clear the roads. The university cancelled all classes. Public transport did not run.

My wife Lyn and I had been married less than a year. Drifts beside the house trailer we rented measured deeper than six feet. For several days we weren't able to leave our trailer park. Being newly-weds, we did not mind.

71

It was while stranded in the snow that I first saw 'Sugar' Ray Leonard box. On the evening news there was an item about him training to fight undisputed champion Wilfredo Benitez for Benitez's world welterweight title. The Benitez–Leonard contest would be broadcast live on Saturday afternoon. I anxiously radared in on the bout. Leonard knocked out the previously unbeaten Benitez in the fifteenth and final round. Leonard's flashy, hands-dropping style indicated that he'd learned much from Ali. But unlike Ali, Leonard seemed no force of nature. There was something in him (something I regarded as disingenuous) that made me dislike him. And I had a fat enough ego to fully believe that, if given the chance, I could entirely humiliate and first-class whup 'Sugar' Ray myself.

But time brings mutations we can't expect. And in the 1980s I became quite a Sugar Ray Leonard fan. When he fights at his best, he's much as Terry Davis describes Pelé in his fine coming-of-age novel, *Vision Quest*. 'He can lift himself, and the rest of us sad-ass human beings, up to a better place, if only for a minute.'

Just a couple of years ago, I finally began making a writing career for myself. Surprisingly to me, three of the first four assignments I wrangled from national magazines were articles about Ray. As I got opportunities to spend time with him, we found we had things in common. When we were kids, we'd both collected comics by the hundreds. As adolescents, we'd worked to emulate Ali and Bruce Lee and we were still big fans of both guys. After we became friendly, I mailed Ray video cassettes of rare Lee footage. When we spent time together, we often spoke about martial arts and discussed a couple little-known facts about Ray's ring skills: he says that he learned much of his defence from watching Bruce Lee movies; and, as Ray trained for fights, during sparring rounds, he often imitated Lee's alleycat-on-heat battle cries.

As Ray was training for what I knew would be one of his very last bouts, I planned to spend several days watching him.

I hoped that he might afford me the opportunity to hop between the ropes and move with him a little.

For the first time in more than a decade, I started seriously training. Throughout October and November, regardless of the weather, early in the afternoons I stepped out to my garage and performed five hard rounds on the heavy bag (only thirty seconds rest between each round), three rounds on the speed bag and shadow-boxed thirty straight minutes per session. In the crisp autumn air, dancing about the bag, trying to rip through its canvas, I'd see Leonard's face in front of me. Not the Ray Charles Leonard I knew as an adult, the one I'd often interviewed and whose ring skills and style I admired – and who I had come to like quite a bit – but my seminal 'Sugar' Ray, the one with the rounded, shining halo of hair, the smarmy attitude and too-cute sailor suits, the one who as a late adolescent I had itched to fight and had felt I might completely humiliate.

That fall, during the months I was training, I found myself doing something else odd: I began dressing to impress Ray Leonard. Although I'm certainly no clothes hound, I bought several elegant jackets and sweaters, many pairs of slacks, dozens of banded-collar shirts, a couple expensive pairs of new street dogs, all in the style and deep ripe colours I had often seen Ray wear.

On 6 December, I packed much of this stuff, and some workout gear, into the back of my old Volvo. I then began the three-hundred-mile drive from Winston-Salem, North Carolina, to Palmer Park, Maryland.

Ray Leonard Road in Palmer Park. A young, skinny, long-legged dog trots between a fading, wine-coloured, velveteen sofa and a rusted-out, mustard-yellow washing machine, both of which have been decorated with green, yellow, red and blue flashing Christmas lights. The dirt-brown hound crosses the road in front of us, turning its head in our direction. It grins supplicatingly, ambles up a knoll, and lifts its leg to a short, white picket fence that encloses two sides of a less than 1,000-square-foot wooden cottage that has been painted a glossy red, white and blue.

'That's it,' says the athlete who has earned more than 110 million dollars from boxing alone. 'That's the one I grew up in.'

We're sitting in the Champ's long, champagne-coloured Mercedes. 'You know what I wanted when I was a kid?' he says. 'I wanted to be a Boy Scout. We couldn't afford the uniforms, the fees. I went to the Goodwill Thrift Shop and they had a uniform. I bought it for fifty cents and wore it everywhere I went. And I was proud. I wore that uniform and told everybody I was a Boy Scout. I wore it so proud.'

As usual, Ray is regally dressed. He's wearing a purple, custom-tailored, double-breasted jacket, a bone-white silk shirt, a pair of soft yellow slacks and purple Chinese-style slippers that have been hand-embroidered with red and gold stitching. This single outfit must have cost as much as his father made in many months when the family was living on this corner.

He wheels the car into the dirt driveway, turns around and drives about half a mile out to the main road. 'You got plans for supper?' he asks. 'I'm going to Mom's. You can come if you want.'

Ray's parents' house is a small, average-looking, brick ranch in a 1970s-style neighbourhood. Average except for the black Rolls-Royce parked in the two-car garage and a big, long, powerful-looking, black speedboat, both of which, Ray says, were once his.

We enter a side door from the garage to the kitchen. Before we find time to remove our jackets, the fighter who for two decades has whipped every opponent who has stepped into the ring with him is pounced on in a way that even Marvellous Marvin Hagler wouldn't dare.

'Ray Charles Leonard,' growls his mother Getha, 'I wish

you'd tell me when you're bringing somebody. All you have to do is pick up the phone.'

Getha Leonard is wearing a red apron and carrying a big wooden spoon, which she's been using to stir a pot on the stove. Ray's dad Cicero is standing at the stove; he, too, is stirring. Like Ray, both parents look younger than their years. Getha Leonard threatens her youngest son with her spoon, but quickly puts it in a pot and shakes hands with me. As Ray introduces us, he tells his mother that I live in North Carolina. She asks if I've been to Wilmington, where Ray was born. I tell her that I lived there for a couple years. 'They want to claim him,' I say. 'The city council'd like to have a parade in his honour.'

Ray ushers me into a small dining room and tells me to take a seat. Soon, steaming platters of fried chicken and biscuits, big white ceramic bowls of rice and summer sausage, a green-bean casserole and a sweating pitcher of sweetened iced tea are placed before us.

The athlete chastises his mother for feeding him fried food. 'Mom, you know I'm in training,' he says. Then he grabs three drumsticks, several biscuits and piles his plate high. When he's downed that, he serves himself seconds.

As we're eating, he asks when I started writing and if I went to school to learn how. I explain that during the time I was teaching martial art, I met a girl who persuaded me to go to university and to try to write a novel.

'Did you marry the girl?' he asks.

'Yes,' I answer, surprised at his question. 'How'd you know?'

'Just figured. It's kinda what happened with Juanita and me. You still married?'

'We married in '78, divorced in 1981, remarried in '84.'

'You married the same girl twice?' he says, sounding astonished, laughing with a hissing sound through his teeth.

'She was the one person who'd put up with me,' I say.

He laughs again, but not so easily. No one says anything for a couple minutes. The air feels heavy as he picks at the scraps on his plate. Finally, he says, 'You know, when I was a kid, I was very, very into myself, withdrawn. I felt I was worthless. When anybody came to the house to visit, I'd go to my room and hide till they left. The first person I didn't hide from was Juanita.'

He stares briefly into the middle distance. 'The gashes are still bleeding,' he says. 'Last Thanksgiving, I was training for Duran and I missed the kids like crazy. This Christmas, they're with me. I asked Jarrel, my six-year-old, what he wanted for Christmas. He said, "I want us to be a family again." Man, that sucks.

'Through all this, I developed a fear of dying. Dying in a plane crash. Praying before I got on and off the plane. I was freaking and nobody knew it. Freaking because I knew I didn't have control.'

We move through the kitchen to a den dominated by a big-screen TV and many poster-sized framed photos of the famous son. Ray slides a video cassette of the last two days' sparring sessions into a VCR. We sit and watch as one of his quick, young sparring partners catches him with a crisp hook and Ray is knocked to the canvas. He rises slowly, shaking his head; his eyes are vacant. He boxes the rest of the round as if his arms and legs are stuck in molasses. Using the remote, Ray rewinds the tape six times, watching the knock-down. 'That won't happen again,' he says finally, studying the knock-down one more time then tugging the cassette from the player but keeping it in his hand.

'Here's the one place I can have control,' he says firmly, speaking more to himself than to me.

Ray and I plan for me to accompany him on his morning roadwork. When I reach his house in Potomac at 6.45, the skies drop; rain falls in nearly horizontal silver sheets. I've brought plenty of Ray Leonard-style uptown sweaters on this trip, but wasn't smart enough to think of rainwear for running. The best I can do is an extra sweatshirt.

After a cold ten minutes of bell ringing, Craig Jones, Ray's personal assistant, answers the door, wearing a pair of boxer shorts and a white tank top. He says to come in and make myself at home in the kitchen; the Champ will be right down. I take a seat at a small breakfast table and look into a large adjoining den. Built-in teak display cases line the whole of the rear wall. Until recently, these were alive with family memorabilia. In the wake of Ray's divorce, they are empty and dusty. An eight-foot, bare, artificial Christmas tree looms in the foyer to my left.

Craig returns, dressed in neon-orange warm-ups. He's carrying a black hooded sweatshirt and a knit cap with a Los Angeles Raiders insignia on it. 'Thought you could use these,' he says.

Ray is close behind him. The three of us are soon standing on the road, smoking out the air in fluorescent-looking clouds and stretching and shadow-boxing to get the juices flowing. The guy I'm hanging out with this morning is the serious Ray Leonard, not the celebrity; there's nothing glitzy in his clothes or countenance – heavy black warm-ups, an old-fashioned longshoreman's cap, a thick, basic black cotton hooded sweatshirt, a pair of new brown work gloves, scuffed leather brogans. Serious boxers don't wear running shoes; work boots strengthen leg muscles and increase stamina.

'How far?' I ask Craig.

'We'll do three,' he answers, meaning miles.

'Hope I can keep up with you,' I say. 'I haven't run in years.'

Craig chuckles. Ray hasn't said a word since we left the house. His features are flat yet attentive; he's tombstone-serious.

Swaddled in proper gear, the December rain feels good on my face; though my glasses are dotted with rain, my vision isn't obstructed. As we run, we throw punches, and we run backwards and sideways for probably half a mile. Ray's face remains almost expressionless. He's gone inward, imagining an opponent, seeing attacks and counters, becoming immortal, gaining control. With about a quarter of a mile to home (his mansion rises out of the fog before us), he opens up in a sprint. I hang with him, stride for stride, until, with about 150 yards left, he drops his transmission into a gear that simply wasn't included with my vehicle.

As we walk around the block to cool down, I'm pleased with this performance. Hell, I had no problem staying with Sugar Ray Leonard until almost the end of his run. And this fall, I haven't been training nearly as hard or as seriously as he has. This feels like the right time to ask my big question.

'Would you consider boxing me a round or so?' I say. 'Today.'

He shakes his head emphatically from side to side. 'No way,' he says, and looks me directly in the face. 'I'd hurt you. I wouldn't mean to . . . but, not now. Not when I'm training. Now, I'd hurt you.'

Today will be Ray's fourth day of sparring for this fight. The windows and doors of the Sugar Ray Leonard Boxing Center in Palmer Park are covered with sheets of fresh white newsprint to stop spectators from peering inside. As I step into the gym, he's already in the ring. There's no play in his demeanour. Black trunks and gloves, his hooded black sweatshirt. He looks the way the older Ray Robinson might've looked, if Robinson had been a Druid.

He paces past me probably a dozen times before he's ready to begin boxing. Although I'm the only person standing ringside, his concentration is such that he does not see me. He peels off the sweatshirt, revealing a plain white T-shirt soaked with sweat and tight, shining, cinnamon-coloured skin on his arms. He continues to pace, luminous and quivering, aching with beauty. Which is to say that although Sugar Ray Leonard is a fine-looking man, he was not born beautiful. Instead of simply being beautiful, he creates his beauty.

It's the first day he's been 'on' in training. Today, he's a ghost in the ring. He boxes with five world-class fighters, none of whom find him. Between rounds, he's jubilant. He and his trainer, Jose 'Pepe' Correa, cannot hide their smiles. 'Beautiful, beautiful,' Correa calls from the apron. 'Yes, yes,' he exclaims as the fighter continues to box with elegance.

When Ray leaves the ring, he blisters the speed bag for several rounds (all the while wearing a less than conscious smile – he's very happy), then polishes off the session with a couple rounds of rope. He then goes with Correa to the exercise table for his abdominal work.

Pepé Correa is tall, long, lean and muscular. At fifty, his hair and moustache are greying. There's street hustler all over his countenance but also mystic. Before Ray begins each exercise, Correa ritualistically closes his eyes, trying to focus his energy, his anima, and place it in his fighter's body. As Ray does hundreds of repetitions, Correa becomes monastically myopic, leaning forward and squinting intently at the movements of every muscle group being used in the particular exercise.

Ray has suffered a bad rope burn in today's sparring. The back of his now translucent T-shirt is streaked with blood. Pepé pulls it away from Ray's body and cuts it from his back with a pair of surgical scissors. He then pulls a bottle of rubbing alcohol from a shelf under the table and pours it directly on to Ray's wound. As the alcohol makes contact, the finest pugilist of the late seventies and early eighties, who has been knocked down so few times in a career of almost two hundred fights and tens of thousands of sparring sessions, drops to his knees, noisily sucking air, working hard to suppress a scream. After Correa finishes, Ray trudges upstairs, slightly bent with pain, to shower. I wait downstairs maybe five minutes, then follow and take a seat on a legless, beat-up, yellow sofa.

'Good run this morning,' he says, stepping from the shower.

'Thanks.'

When he's through towelling off, Ray pulls on a one-piece olive military jumpsuit and a pair of black shiny combat boots. 'You bring any Bruce stuff with you?' he asks.

I have a tape in the car, I tell him.

'When I'm in training,' he says, 'I learn from Bruce Lee. He gets me energised, makes me more explosive. I'll let you in on something I've never told anybody,' he continues, taking a seat beside me and bending to lace his boots. 'When I was a kid, I used to come back from Bruce movies and go into my mom's backyard. He fired me up so much I took my fist and drove it into the ground until I made a hole three or four inches deep.'

He doesn't look embarrassed by his admission. I unabashedly tell him I did similar things myself. Then we stand and walk downstairs. As we step into the main gym, I say, 'You had your legs under you today. Pretty soon, you'll be a totally tuned man.'

'Wait and see,' he says. 'In another two weeks I'll be able to catch guys with right hands like this.'

There's a wall a half-step to our left. In one movement, he falls to the plaster, slapping his shoulders against it, rocks on his heels for leverage and, rolling forward to his toes, springs a heaven-and-hell of a punch a couple inches past the right side of my jaw. As he rips the right, he allows the momentum to carry him behind me, where there's no way I'd be able to counter – as if I'd be standing to even think about it.

I spin and look at him. His eyes are hard-bright. 'Watch this,' he says, snaking his open right hand past my raised left fist, but very slowly now, gently, across the shoulder and behind my neck, which he lightly clasps. His hand is as small as a woman's. The act is tender, a seeming gesture of friendship. Until he pulls my head down into a crisp left uppercut, which he stops a quarter-inch from my chin. I'm stunned by the heat I feel coming from him.

'After that, you could try this,' he says, powdering the air

80

in front of my hips and abdomen with a patented Sugar Ray body combination. I don't see the punches, but feel the pressure of the air as it dusts my torso.

'For me, that wouldn't be natural,' I say, forcing myself to speak, pretending not to be in awe.

'What would *you* do?' he asks, moving back a little and watching me closely. He's testing – he intends to find out exactly what I know about his art.

'I think I'd try to angle a hook over here, maybe push him off like this, probably jab behind it to finish the combination or open him up for something else.'

I place my palms high on Ray's chest and shove him back about eighteen inches. He keeps good position and balance.

But in the act of pushing Sugar Ray Leonard, I have now gone with him to a world beyond words, to a universe so intimate, honest and immediate – and so dangerously between two people – that, even with my ambitious ego in high gear and my long-ago ring experience, it just about scares the leaves off my tree.

I see the look he wants to hide (he lowers a reptilian lid inside his eyes) but can't. He's wearing a hard, ever-so-slight smile. This says that something in the way I've pushed him has told him more about my limitations and abilities than he could have learned through many hours of verbal sparring. In the interminable moments of facing off, fighters never want opponents to know what they can and cannot do. In this way, making war is always about lying to the man in front of you. But now, whether or not I like it (and I damned well don't), I am standing naked in front of Sugar Ray Leonard.

'I need to tell you something,' I say, having no clue what words will come from my mouth. 'I used to not like you,' I say. 'And I couldn't admit it was because I was envious. In a way, I wanted to be who you were. I guess now I don't need that any more.'

He gives me a look only slightly less than stunned. Then he studies me dead on; finally, his eyes soften. 'Hey, man, ain't no thing,' he says, clapping a hand on my shoulder. 'With what I do, you get used to not being liked. Say, tell you what . . . how about you come to Mom's again tonight and we'll chow down on some Chinese food?'

I accept Ray's offer with weak knees and considerable relief.

The Thursday after this story was published in Ray's home-town newspaper, the Washington Post, *I found myself seated ringside at Madison Square Garden as thirty-five-year-old Ray Leonard challenged young, hard-hitting, carnivorous speedster Terry Norris for Norris's world super-welterweight crown. In dramatic contrast to every other fight in Ray's championship career, the arena was mostly empty; there were less than 7,000 people in attendance. The light was grey-green and murky, the big famous room dank and quiet. Ray entered the ring blinking at the lights; his skin was tinted a dull green. From the beginning of the first round, he looked scared yet resigned and he moved so slowly it seemed as if he was trying to fight from underwater. Norris, who considered Ray to be his stylistic mentor, badly beat up my friend. I saw Ray age fifteen years in the first five minutes of the bout. After the second round, staring at the shining green-tinged concrete floor near my feet because I didn't want to watch the ring, I recognised that I was staying in the arena because I felt an obligation – to Ray – similar to one I'd felt a couple of years before, when I'd sat through much of the night with my younger cousin Steve in a hospital emergency room. Steve had been riding his bicycle home from work on a Friday afternoon when he'd been hit by a car he did not see coming.*

In the Garden, that penultimate shrine of boxing history where Ray had never fought and I had never written about a fight, Norris knocked two of Ray's centre bottom teeth down his throat, cracked and splintered several ribs on his right

82

side, and generally darkened and reshaped his face in a way that looked as if it might be permanent. (It was a much more frightening – yet humanising – experience sitting six feet from this event than it would have been staring at it on a television screen.) Ray did not win a single minute of the fight, but made it through to the end of the twelfth and final round, chiefly because Norris had taken it easy on his idol. As the long foregone decision was announced, both Norris and Ray looked apologetic and embarrassed.

Walking to the post-fight press conference, I watched newspaper reporters, some young and inexperienced, others having travelled with Ray throughout his long amateur and professional careers. Almost every person I watched and listened to seemed basically unaffected by what they'd witnessed. Within a year, I had made the commitment I'd needed to make for a while – to stop writing glorifying boxing stories for magazines and for newspapers.

BRUCE LEE, AMERICAN

Esquire, September 1993; *Men's Journal*, February 1997; *Panorama* (Australia), July 1997; *M Quarterly* (Japan), October 1997; *Esquire*, September 1998; *Arena*, October 1998; *Winston-Salem Journal*, 17 November 1998; *Independent on Sunday*, 5 December 1999; *Hotdog*, April 2001.

This essay began largely as a 'I can't take it any more; please let me tell an honest story' reaction to the worst professional experience I've had as a writer – working on the abysmal Warner Brothers documentary, Curse of the Dragon, *with Fred Weintraub, who produced Bruce Lee's last movie,* Enter the Dragon. *If trying to write a good book is like swimming at sea, and writing a good movie is like swimming in the bath, then 'writing' with Fred Weintraub is like trying to step barefooted around a bacteria-ridden puddle. To read more about my misadventures on that project and with Fred, please see my book* The Tao of Bruce Lee. *I wrote 'Bruce Lee, American' in the spring of 1993, starting work on the story within days of having completed my role in Fred's* Curse. *Six years later, this essay served as part of the core of* The Tao of Bruce Lee, *although until this volume, more than thirty per cent of the original draft has never been published.*

Thanks to Chris Marriott at bruceleedivinewind.cjb.net for his support of this story and for his friendship.

'I DIDN'T KNOW his life had so much . . . well, depth to it,' says one of many college-looking boys cloistered in a loose circle near the exit from the shopping mall cinema lobby.

'Don't you think they ended it too soon?' suggests the cynic of the bunch, the one smoking an unfiltered cigarette.

'Well, they couldn't show how he died,' says one with sun-bleached hair and an untried face. 'His heart blew up,' the kid explains, as surely as if he had been in the room when this event took place twenty years earlier.

'Is that what he died of?' asks another of the boys. 'Is that what killed Bruce Lee?'

'That's right, his heart couldn't take the strain.'

'Nah, man, I heard it was his brain,' says yet another lad. 'It was his brain that blew up.'

'Well, whatever blew up, it was because it couldn't take the strain.'

Several boys nod knowingly. They're satisfied. The particulars are unimportant, the details insignificant. The physical cause of death for the thirty-two-year-old, self-proclaimed world's fittest man doesn't matter. What's understood is that the cause of Bruce Lee's death, whatever it may have been, was directly related to his martial art and his extraordinary athletic skills. The point of the mythology is this: Bruce Lee had gone places we aren't supposed to go, had looked into the abyss and then been devoured by it. The college boys understand this, without possessing the words to say so. We all understand.

Fame as faceless as God.

Few people have attained this, the ultimate, ethicless, unqualified fame. Among the names that come to mind: Jesus, Buddha, Mohammed.

Should our species survive for several hundred more years, our fame-driven century will have spawned other, arrogantly secular, American gods: Muhammad Ali, Elvis Presley and, yes, Bruce Lee – a name that will pass into international mythology as 'the greatest martial warrior of all time', a folk hero whose 'deeds' will be recounted as pure fiction.

Surprisingly, the name Bruce Lee may be known in more places than that of anyone else of the twentieth century. He's idolised in New York, London and Paris; emulated by martial artists in India, Lebanon and Brazil; his likeness hangs in mud huts in central African nations and on apartment walls in Kiev; he's honoured by devotees in Detroit and LA, as well as in Tokyo, Cleveland, Beijing and Mexico City.

The movie that the college boys and I had been watching was *Dragon: The Bruce Lee Story*. 'Director Rob Cohen . . . does right by Bruce Lee,' John Anderson wrote for *Newsday*, 'making the movie about Bruce Lee that Bruce Lee might have made himself.' Mike Clark, writing in *USA Today* said, 'The last pop bio this much fun to watch [was] *The Buddy Holly Story*.'

My feelings about *Dragon* are less enthralled, partly because I know something about Lee's real life, the one that most reviewers didn't bother to research and that Cohen and the producers and writers of *Dragon* saw as not dramatic (obvious) enough for their film. Lee's widow, Linda, having been paid handsomely for the rights to her dead husband's story – and allowed considerable sterilising control – lovingly embraced and endorsed her own and Cohen's saccharin-sweetened lollipop.

'I probed what was memorable about Bruce Lee's life,' Cohen claimed, 'and discovered that he was a warrior, a philosopher, a husband, a father, a teacher, a writer and a thinker. Ultimately, he did all these things with perfectionist zeal.'

Why is it then that Cohen's specious product bears little real relationship to Bruce Lee's life and art? Indeed, *Dragon* seems to have been influenced most by not Lee but Hong Kong and Taiwanese movies of a generation before, the ones that dramatically damaged Lee's reputation in the years following his death and that had such titles as *Bruce Lee*

Strikes Back from the Grave, The Clones of Bruce Lee and *Bruce Lee Goes to Hell*, and that starred a legion of self-parodying androids such as Bruce Li, Bruce Le, Bruce Lei, Bruce LeRoy, Myron Bruce Lee, Dragon Lee, (Charles) Bronson Lee, Brute Lee, Bruce Tease, Spruce Trees, Loose Leaves.

Cohen's film, *Dragon*, is distinguished from earlier exploitations mostly in these ways: it is silicone slick, many reviewers enjoyed it and it creates yet another layer of silly pop legend that minimises Lee's actual life and concretises his reputation.

For twenty years, I've been fascinated with Lee and have found him to be a flawed, complex, yet singular talent whose reputation has been even more abused than Elvis's – the basic facts of Presley's life have been reported hundreds of times. The mist of money-making myth around Lee is so thick that the truth of his story has been almost entirely obscured.

The reality is this: Lee's snap-shot brief life was rich and fascinating; to fictionalise it is to reduce it. In a few short years, Lee single-fistedly revolutionised the martial arts and for ever changed action movie-making. Along the way, he became the first truly international film luminary. So far, he has received little credit for these accomplishments.

Consider Gatsby and his optimistic, orderly, yet doomed pursuit of the dream. A great literary figure begins to emerge, in the way that Ali and Elvis are characters of consequence – something in the belly, blood and bones of these lives elevates biography into apologue. The place to start looking at Lee in this way is at the beginning.

The beginning for me (and for millions of others around the world) was in September 1973, when its subject had been in his grave for nearly two months. I was a drowsy-eyed, twenty-one-year-old freshman at a junior college in the mountain village of Banner Elk, North Carolina. It was a miserable time in my life. I was five-foot-seven and weighed ninety pounds. In high school, guys had nicknamed me 'Foetus'. Although most of my contemporaries were preparing to graduate from university and proceed into the real world, I was maturing slowly if (and there was real doubt about this) I was growing up at all.

That September marked the first time I'd been away from my father's house for longer than a weekend. I was homesick. To relieve my misery, I spent time in Banner Elk's only movie house, a place about the size of, and maybe half as clean as, a greasy old two-car garage.

The movie that night was *Enter the Dragon*. As I found a springy, worn-out seat in the centre of the second row, the house lights dimmed, the mouldering, wine-coloured velvet curtains parted, the blood-red Warner Brothers logo flashed on to the screen.

And then, in that oversized room where dreams prowl, he appeared like a lighted window in a darkened wall. Everything else blurred into the background. The air crackled as the camera panned in close and he grew in the centre of the screen, luminous with sweat and hubris.

One minute into the movie, Bruce Lee threw his first punch. With it, a power came roiling up from Lee's abdomen, affecting itself in blistering waves not only upon his onscreen opponent, but on the movie audience.

A wind blew through me. My hands shook; I quivered electrically from head to toe, as if I'd swallowed a belly full of lightning. And then Bruce Lee launched the first *real* kick I had ever seen. My jaw fell open like the business end of a dump truck. This man could fly. Not like Superman – better – his hands and his feet flew whistling through sky. Yes, better: this wasn't simply a shadow-box fantasy; there was a seed of reality in every Lee movement, the essence of something much more real than anything or anyone I had seen on a movie screen. Yet to watch Lee felt just like a dream.

For the next ninety-three minutes, everything was as blinding, noisy, and insanely beautiful as digitally enhanced film of a desert nuclear weapons blast.

Neutron bomb Bruce Lee was unlike anyone I (or any of us) had experienced.

Unlike other Hollywood action performers, the seed of reality was in his every movement. Part of the appeal for me was that he was only about my size: though he seemed nearly invulnerable, he was short, grassblade thin, almost puny; there was a fragility, an eggshell mortality, about him.

At the end of *Enter the Dragon*, I looked at the world around me for the first time since Lee had appeared on screen. Compared to the song his body had sung, my life was cold, mechanical, tedious. A Holden Caulfield whine.

I had no illusions about *Enter the Dragon* being a great or even a good film. It wasn't the movie itself that had so affected me; it was Bruce Lee, who transcended the film. When I stumbled across Lee in *Enter the Dragon*, I felt that my discovery could be paralleled to finding an ancient Taoist scroll in the bargain bin at a small-town five-and-dime.

Over the next five years, I would study *Enter the Dragon* and Lee's other three films dozens of times. In 1973 and 1974, Lee movies were shown in middle-class shopping malls, but by the mid-seventies, in search of enlightenment, I'd descend into the dank, cool confines of dilapidated inner-city cinemas, the air reeking of piss and Thunderbird wine. I'd take my seat among a couple dozen screaming, screeching black folks, a few Occidental street toughs, and maybe a drunk old boogie-man who'd wake from his catatonia, jump from his seat and yell, 'Kill that muhfucka,' whenever characters stopped talking and Lee hit someone.

Twenty years later, I tell this story not as simple memoir or as self-revelation, but because I believe it says much about Lee's screen image, the dream he developed, and the innate, supremely powerful effect he had (and continues to have) on his core audience: the lonely, the frustrated, the inarticulate, the disaffected, the downtrodden, the half-asleep. This dead man who, at least on celluloid, Kodachrome, in magazines and more recently on home video, was more alive than anyone I had met.

We have the impression, when watching his movies, that he arrived fully actualised, that he had always been Bruce Lee, the god of martial art. But even Hemingway's leopard, 'dried and frozen' near the western summit of Kilimanjaro, must have worked to reach the altitude at which he finally fell, beautiful and damned.

Lee was born in San Francisco in 1940 – the year of the dragon. His parents named him Li Jun Fan and legend has it that a nurse arbitrarily entered the Christian name Bruce Lee on his birth certificate.

His mother, Grace, was half German; his father, Li Hoi Chuen, a popular and wealthy Hong Kong comic actor (in *Dragon*, Lee's father was anonymous and nearly impoverished), was touring the United States as a star performer with a highly regarded Peking opera company. The elder Li arranged his son's first movie role: Bruce Lee appeared in a Hong Kong picture when he was three weeks old.

Lee grew up on the Kowloon side of Hong Kong with two brothers, two sisters, a pet monkey and several servants. The adolescent Bruce Lee had a high energy level and a propensity for getting into trouble. His family's Cantonese nickname for him translates as 'Never Sits Still'.

Although most fans think of Lee as the character we see in *Enter the Dragon* – a man alone, completely attuned to the natural world and his inner rhythms, a man clean of secondary wisdom – the real Lee admired and was influenced not by solitary Shaolin monks but by American pop stars such as Elvis, James Dean and Jerry Lewis (all of whom are observable in his martial arts movie performances), and by Chinese movies about martial arts masters. By his eighteenth year, Lee had starred in twenty films, none of them about martial arts, and he was a major teen idol in Hong Kong.

At thirteen, he began to study wing chun gung fu. Movie

lore has it that he was a quick and obsessive student. The truth is that he was more interested in acting and in dancing (he was the cha-cha champion of Hong Kong) and didn't take serious interest in wing chun until years later. 'Bruce was a rebel,' claims Hawkins Cheung, who studied gung fu with Lee. 'He learned to fight on the streets, not in wing chun class. Gangs fought with knives, metal pipes, bicycle chains. We hid razor blades in our shoes. Between 1950 and 1960, Hong Kong teenagers were very violent. Everybody wanted to be fast like American gunslingers in western movies. Bruce was the fastest of everybody. When we were looking for a fight, it was easy. Walk a couple of blocks, that's all it took. Bruce was a child star, everybody recognised him. It was easy.'

As is true of many people who make their livelihoods from martial arts, Cheung is a legendiser: his comments are more myth than reality. But they are useful in this way: to indicate what Lee disciples believe they 'know' about their idol – and how incorrect much of this belief is. According to accepted Lee ideology, in his late teens, the future god of gung fu fought not only on street corners and in alleys, but in organised, yet illegal, rooftop contests. (Fact, however, is this: Lee's own martial arts teacher, Wong Shun Leung, says he knows of only one contest the teenage Bruce Lee was involved in – it was a supervised, controlled sparring situation and no one was injured.) In folklore, in Lee's last teenage battle, his opponent's skull was fractured. When police knocked on the door of Li Hoi Chuen asking questions, the elder Li, who had a considerable reputation to maintain, saved face, and Bruce Lee's life, by banishing his privileged, street-fighting, movie-star son to the United States.

The truth of how Bruce Lee came to the US is a bit more mundane. His father felt that the boys who 'Never Sits Still' was beginning to hang out with were bad influences. To learn more positive ways of being in the world, he sent his son to San Francisco to live with upstanding family friends.

Lee's adjustment to life in the US was not unconventional

for a Hong Kong immigrant. Within weeks of arriving in San Francisco, he moved to Seattle, where he struggled to improve his English and graduate from high school at Edison Technical Institute. He eventually attended the University of Washington as a less than scholarly philosophy student. 'He went around puffing himself up and doing push-ups in front of everybody,' says Amy Sanbo, his first US girlfriend and fellow philosophy major. 'Philosophy students made fun of him and called him "Beefcake". He got other people to write his papers for him – one of his gung fu students, Ed Hart, and a guy he lived with, Shelton Chow.'

Before nearly flunking out of, and finally quitting, university in his third year, he found another girlfriend, got her pregnant and married her – not the sexually aggressive genius cheerleader in *Dragon*, but a timid and inexperienced, perpetually puzzled, sweet- and sleepy-looking coed named Linda Emery who often sat beside Lee, silently mouthing his words as he spoke. Lee's wife looks not like Lauren Holly, the chesty and suntanned starlet who played the role of Linda in *Dragon*, but Shelly Duvall. 'When I look at photos of Bruce and Linda together,' says George Tan, a documentary movie-maker and the world's premier expert on Lee's life, films and martial art, 'him and those huge-ass forearms, her all long-limbed, repressed and gawky, I see Popeye and Olive Oyl.'

At gung fu demonstrations in Seattle, Lee attracted similar folks to those who would later become his most obsessive movie fans. 'Tough guys *and* wimps flocked to Bruce,' says Jesse Glover, Lee's first-ever martial arts student.

Although *Dragon* perpetrates the Lee myth that he was a ready, anxious and brilliant martial arts instructor, the historical Lee was at best a reluctant teacher. 'He wasn't interested and he didn't have the patience,' explains James DeMile, another of Lee's Seattle students. 'He used us to improve his own skills, which isn't the same as teaching. There were guys he kept around just to use as human punching bags.'

Upon leaving Seattle, the Lee family spent an eventful stint in Oakland. In February 1965, a son Brandon was born, like his father, in the year of the dragon. Lee opened a gung fu school in San Francisco's Chinatown. In the 1960s, gung fu was basically unknown to the West; Chinese practitioners were secretive and clannish. Lee's teaching methods were distinct and unorthodox; he taught all ethnic groups, taught only what he considered usable street-fighting techniques, he and his students wore regular clothes (no uniforms) when they practised, and he had no ranking system (his students wore no black and coloured belts). When elders in San Francisco's Chinese community discovered that Lee was teaching outside the 'family', they sent a representative to confront him. 'He came into Bruce's school,' explains Dan Inosanto, a long-time Lee student. 'This guy said, "If you beat me, you can teach non-Chinese. If I beat you, you gotta close your school."'

In *Dragon*, this encounter is recreated as a high-kicking duel to the death between two athletes who are as hard-bodied and vibrant as agitated yellowjackets. Lee is paralysed by his evil, dirty-fighting opponent and becomes depressed until he is coaxed from his funk by the always beautiful and eternally optimistic Linda, who persuades him to write a philosophical treatise about his martial art that is published almost overnight and becomes a mainstream bestseller. This Hollywood revision trivialises not only Lee's life but his effect on martial arts. Before Lee, the vast majority of martial practitioners were basically incapable of defending themselves; in addition, athletes as we think of them in the West simply didn't exist in the Chinese fighting arts.

World champion kick-boxing pioneer Don 'the Dragon' Wilson says of his first ring fight, which took place in 1974, 'I was so scared I was shaking. I honestly thought that when I hit somebody or he hit me, the one who got caught first would be killed on the spot. That's pretty much what everybody thought back in those days, before we knew that's not the way it works. Nobody had ever really tried all this "lethal" karate shit before we did.'

In the real-world version of Lee's Oakland scrap, his timid, runty and underqualified opponent turned and ran as he was chased around a room. With closed fists (because he didn't have the experience to know better), Lee pounded the back of his challenger's head until his own hands became swollen and he was exhausted and gasping for breath. Lee then tackled his opponent, pinned his arms down, sat on him, and asked if he was ready to say 'uncle'.

Although Lee had won this anticlimactic variation of a schoolyard tussle, in the process he found wing chun to be fairly ineffective, and his own physical conditioning wanting, which brought on a period of considerable introspection. With what was as much an obsession for success as a passion for knowledge (in a very real way, it didn't matter to Lee whether he earned a living as an actor, a dancer or as a martial artist – he simply wanted to make a level of money that would approximate his personal arrogance), he began a process of nearly endless reading, ruminating and training: he made a decision that he was going to become the best martial artist in the history of the world.

As if by osmosis, Bruce 'Never Sits Still' Lee had adopted the distinctly American faith: that we can invent ourselves on a daily basis. And that we can work to become whatever and whoever we wish.

Over the next several years, Lee arguably became the first Western-style athlete in the martial disciplines. He ran, pushed weights, jumped rope, performed calisthenics, punched bags, developed dozens of pieces of personal-training equipment that he used daily (some of which, after his death, became accepted martial arts training aids). 'No one ever trained as fanatically as Bruce,' says Chuck Norris, who was one of Lee's students. 'He seemed to train twenty-four hours a day.'

It was this ongoing trip into the internal wilderness that

would be the basis of the revolution that Lee would lead in the martial arts.

He gave a demonstration of his method, which he called Jun Fan gung fu (named after himself), at a karate tournament in Los Angeles. Celebrity hairdresser Jay Sebring, who would soon become a student of Lee's, took film of that demo to *Batman* television producer William Dozier, who called Lee in for a screen test and eventually cast him as Kato in *The Green Hornet* TV series.

The Lee family moved to Los Angeles, where a daughter, Shannon, was born and there was one season of *The Green Hornet*. Respected veteran stuntman Gene LeBell, who regularly worked on the show, derisively describes Lee's role: 'Bruce was a driver that drove the star around and wore a black outfit and a little hat.'

Lee himself was not keen on his co-star role in *The Green Hornet*. He wanted to make 'real' movies, be a 'real' star. Although he was frustrated by the robotics of playing Kato (before and since Lee, martial arts characters on TV and in the movies have always been less than human and little more than fighting robots, even when cast in lead parts) and his subsequent lack of acting jobs, he didn't despair. Linda took a job as a secretary, which allowed her ambitious husband the opportunity to commit himself yet more rigorously to his aspiration of becoming the world's most complete fighter.

'She gave him what he wanted,' explains James Coburn, who was a friend, benefactor and one of Lee's Los Angeles pupils. 'She left him alone, gave him comfort when he needed it, had children, and did everything for them. It kept him free. There was a kind of Asian subservience to it.'

Where almost all martial arts practitioners in the world slavishly followed one style of combat or another, Lee analysed and taught himself not only parts of dozens of Eastern combat systems, including gung fu, karate, tae kwon do, judo and ju-jitsu, but also Western boxing, wrestling and fencing. Wing chun has few kicking techniques; the kicks that

Lee knew, and wisely would have used in combat, were thrown to the knees and groin. He began developing not only superior street-fighting skills, but also an alternate, spectacular, high-kicking movie martial art. Says Coburn, 'Bruce sucked up everything he could apply to his art. If it worked, it worked. If it didn't, out it went.'

Lee began calling his street-fighting method 'jeet kune do', which translates as 'way of the intercepting fist'. Eventually, though, he regretted giving his art a name. 'I am all styles, yet I am no style,' he said. He had labelled, and thereby limited, that which he thought of as limitless, formless, beyond definition.

'He says JKD has no technique,' Inosanto notes. 'My wife says everybody in the sixties talked that way.' Like all of us, the 'limitless, formless' Bruce Lee was an ambiguous character driven by his biology, his acculturation and his time: the late sixties and early seventies, that phase when self-invention – the notion that you can cut yourself loose from psychic and physical moorings and float free, beyond the pull of gravity – seemed most possible.

On a trip to Bombay with Coburn, Lee visited a school that taught a traditional Indian martial art. The class hadn't heard of Lee, but after he gave an impromptu demonstration dressed in street clothes, the instructor and students bowed to him on hands and knees. One can't feed two kids and a wife, though, simply by being the god of gung fu. And the unemployed actor found it necessary to return to his role as martial arts instructor, with which he was now thoroughly bored.

One reason Lee felt that he couldn't seriously commit to, and was disinterested in, teaching martial arts classes is that he desperately wanted to showcase his mushrooming skills before a larger audience. He would educate the entire world to Eastern culture and his ideas of what the martial arts *should* be (while validating his own shining existence). Bruce Lee, our twentieth-century positivist, knew just one place to seize this shimmering future.

The place he knew was the perfect, the obvious, *the only*! vehicle that could transport his martial art to the world. Bruce Lee, child of the movies, whose ideals of a gung fu master came straight from films he'd loved as a child, made the decision to pursue his singular art in this singular way: he would become the world's best-known martial artist by becoming the first genuinely international movie star. 'In the history of movies, there's never been anyone else like Bruce,' says George Tan. 'If Clint Eastwood had been a sheriff who became Christian about the whole thing and wanted to show real sheriffing and chose movies as the medium, you could compare that to Bruce Lee.'

From 1967 through 1971, Lee taught many notables in the film community, including Coburn, Steve McQueen, directors Roman Polanski and Blake Edwards, influential screenwriter Stirling Silliphant and Warner Brothers president Ted Ashley. For those connected to the industry, those shepherds of the shimmering dream, Bruce Lee became the ideal of the martial monk, the wise man of gung fu.

'Bruce's interest in philosophising grew enormously when he decided he needed to develop an image, a device to market his martial art,' says Tan. As Lee had incorporated elements from gung fu, boxing, judo, karate, etc., to create his fighting methods, he looked to the writings of gurus of the sixties to develop 'his' philosophy. He particularly admired anti-mystic Jiddu Krishnamurti, who at the age of ten in southern India had been adopted by elders of the Theosophical Society, a mystical order that took him to be a reincarnated embodiment of the Hindu god Krishna. At thirty-four, Krishnamurti renounced the Theosophists (but not his role as 'World Messenger') and spent the remainder of his ninety-one years delivering the message that the very separatist nature of religions and organised schools of thought are impediments to truth.

Aphorisms attributed to Lee and now religiously quoted by his widow, former students and thousands of followers were lifted directly from Krishnamurti's work. 'Truth is not something dictated by your pleasure or pain,' wrote Krishnamurti, 'or by your conditioning as a Hindu or whatever religion you belong to. The man who is really serious, with the urge to find out what truth is, what love is, has no concept at all. He lives only in what is.'

In *The Tao of Jeet Kune Do*, a collection of notes Lee wrote for his own purposes and never intended to publish, but which were, posthumously, by his still-enthralled, not wealthy widow, Bruce Lee wrote, 'Fighting is not something dictated by your conditioning as a kung fu man, a karate man, a judo man or what not. The man who is really serious, with the urge to find out what truth is, has no [martial arts] style at all. He lives only in what is.'

To say that Bruce Lee was not a great thinker, that he claimed others' thoughts as his own partly as a marketing ploy, is not to suggest that he didn't take these 'non-ideas' seriously. 'I saw Bruce as a renegade Taoist priest,' says basketball legend Kareem Abdul Jabbar, another of Lee's Los Angeles students. 'He was into spirituality and it was heavily influenced by Taoism. But you couldn't put him in that box, he was beyond all that.'

'Fighting, as is, is simple and total,' Lee wrote in *Black Belt* magazine. 'The core of understanding lies in the individual mind, and until that is touched everything is uncertain and superficial. Truth cannot be perceived until we come to fully understand ourselves and our potentials. After all, knowledge in the martial arts ultimately means self-knowledge.'

In the years since Lee's death, the notion that we can be whatever we want, that we can liberate ourselves, has become the stuff of television commercials. In the early 1970s, the concept of self-actualisation looked shining, innocent and new.

The aggressively self-actualised Bruce Lee used movie industry students to try to convince powerful Hollywood producers that martial arts scenes would have more sizzle than ham-fisted John Wayne-style film fights. No one took him seriously enough to give him a chance as a star.

'Never sits still.' Never gives up. Lee had a story idea called *The Warrior* about a Shaolin priest's adventures in the American West, which he took to friends at Warner Brothers, who liked the idea and wrangled production money to create a ninety-minute pilot for television. 'He came into my office swinging his nunchuks and jumping up and down for what must've been ten minutes,' says former Warner Brothers television executive Tom Kuhn. 'We never seriously considered him for the role.'

Lee's story idea eventually became the *Kung-fu* TV series, which, in the dubious tradition of Fu Manchu, Charlie Chan and Mr Moto, starred Caucasian, drug-doing, non-martial artist David Carradine as Chinese gung fu master Kwai Chang Caine, the role that the world's most relentlessly conditioned Chinese martial artist had conceived for himself.

In April 1970, Lee returned to Hong Kong to visit his mother and brother Robert (his father had died in 1965). For the first time, *The Green Hornet* series was playing in Hong Kong and Lee was surprised to find that he was something of a celebrity, a minor home-town hero. He had left Hong Kong a well-known trouble child and had returned transformed, enlightened, a master of a new form of gung fu, a local boy who had 'made good' on the fabled Gold Mountain of Hollywood. Lee appeared on the popular Hong Kong TV talk show, *Enjoy Yourself Tonight*, where he gave an extraordinarily commanding demonstration of his martial art.

That performance was brought to the attention of the head of Hong Kong's fledgling and floundering Golden Harvest studios, Raymond Chow, who was desperate for a hit picture. Not long after Lee returned to Los Angeles from Hong Kong (and at almost exactly the time that he realised he would always be treated as a third-world citizen in Hollywood), Chow offered a two-picture deal of $7,500 per movie that Lee would eventually accept.

Bruce Lee's success occurred with the suddenness of a streaking meteorite seen through a keyhole. With the release of his first movie, *The Big Boss*, he immediately became as big a celebrity in Hong Kong as the Beatles had been in 1963 in Britain. In addition, his movies shattered box-office records throughout south-east Asia. In Singapore, showings were postponed because of traffic jams caused by fans.

The reason for such powerful reactions: 'Even in those crudely made pictures, his vitality was extraordinary,' says Fred Weintraub, who co-produced *Enter the Dragon*. 'The life force was just staggering. No one had ever seen anything like Bruce before.'

He brought his wife and children to Hong Kong from Los Angeles. After they'd settled in, he all but ignored them. Says Tan, 'He was getting all the adulation he could want from other people. He had alternate sources of affection, a lot of girlfriends.'

Hong Kong women found Lee irresistible. They saw him as worldly, mysterious, scholarly, as the equivalent of the male ideal in Western romance novels. Lee's lovers included his female co-stars. He bought a floor-length fur coat, Elvis-style sunglasses, a red Mercedes convertible.

Larry Tan, who would later choreograph martial arts fights for several American films, including *Remo Williams* and *The Wanderers*, describes a 1972 meeting with his childhood idol. 'I'd expected a warrior-monk and what I got was Mr Vegas. He was this smart little man who had transformed himself onscreen into a physical giant, but he was an emotional midget. His cologne – it was so overpowering I smelled him before I saw him. He was coming down a set of steps from a restaurant and the first thing I saw was this pair of four-inch elevator heels. He was wearing bell-bottoms, this big lapelled leather jacket and bright flowered shirt, huge sunglasses. He was so tiny. I couldn't believe how small his hands and wrists were.'

In mid-1972, the idol of Hong Kong wrote, co-produced

and directed the supposedly autobiographical *Way of the Dragon*, in which the wealthy childhood star played a country bumpkin; in addition, he choreographed fights, dubbed English voices to the Mandarin soundtrack and played percussion for the score. Privately, he experimented with complex rhythms of Hindu music, hoping to apply them to the flow of combat and of fight-scene choreography, tried electric shock to speed his reaction time, had the sweat glands removed from under his arms because he didn't like the way his dripping pits looked onscreen, drove open fingers into closed steel cans of cola. He told friends that, before the end of 1973, he'd be able to plunge his fingers through pine boards, a feat which had surely never been accomplished; after his death, boards would be found in his home with dramatic indentations in the wood.

His reputation as a transcendent martial warrior was growing, though not everyone was wowed. Rick Thomas, a former mercenary soldier in Africa and South America, was working in Hong Kong, dubbing villains' voices in movies. 'I'd known Bruce for a while,' he says. 'I went to try out for a part in *Way of the Dragon*, the movie where he fought Chuck Norris. Bruce was showing me his stuff, throwing a bunch of flippy, flashy kicks. I stuck my finger out and tapped him on the chest. "Bruce, I could hit you right here," I said, "and both your arms would fall off." Needless to say, I didn't get the part.'

Lee began receiving movie offers from around the world and bragged that he'd become an emissary for global harmony. Bruce Lee, the bringer of internationalism, the harbinger of one-world culturisation that must take place in the twenty-first century.

Never sits still. Always reinventing. He wanted his next movie, *Game of Death*, to be an action movie/philosophical thesis about the value of adaptability as a warrior, as well as a person. He wrote in letters to friends that he planned to divorce Linda and would return to live in LA. 'He'd been drinking cow blood,' says Coburn, who visited Lee in Hong Kong in late 1972, 'spun in the blender, running seven miles a day. His skin was like very thin velvet – you could see every muscle and every muscle, of course, was absolutely workable. It was like he could leap twenty feet in the air and stick on the wall and come down. That shining glowing velvet skin. He looked beautiful.'

I am all styles; yet I am no style. 'I use no way as way, have no limitation as limitation,' said Lee.

Bruce Lee was movie star, writer, stunt choreographer, director, producer, philosopher, revolutionary, little man's Messiah. In his quest to become the complete person, warrior and healer, monk and lover, creature of intellect, flesh and spirit, he felt the need to be the best in the world at any (and almost every) thing he undertook.

Then, something began to go terribly, inexplicably wrong with the Great God Muscle he'd spent his obsessive life building.

We see: Lee removing his shirt before his fight scene with Chuck Norris in *Way of the Dragon*. There's an aura around him; he glows. Next, we see: Lee in the opening fight from *Enter the Dragon*, the last scene filmed for the movie. He's painfully thin, almost spindly, his skin looks stretched tight, his forehead is distended, and he moves stiffly, mechanically. He's a figure in an El Greco painting – angular, elongated, ready to ascend into heaven.

There were numerous newspapers in Hong Kong and Lee was prominently featured in each of them almost every day. When he wanted to go for a drive to relax, he was escorted by motorcycle police. To prevent riots, when he went to buy clothing, department stores closed and he shopped by himself. It was a by-product of Lee's martial training to be purposely paranoid. For years, he'd worked at being aware of movements of people who might attack him, to size up everyone in crowds. The eminently self-actualised Bruce Lee's martial arts fanaticism did not prepare him for the noose of hyper-celebrity in a small, densely crowded city.

Since his Hollywood days, when Steve McQueen introduced him to smoking marijuana, Lee had been an occasional
recreational drug user. Now, in hopes of calming himself and
relieving the choking level of stress he felt that he was under,
he regularly ate hashish and leaves of marijuana, choosing not
to smoke the drugs because he didn't want to damage his
health.

There was greater paranoia, sleeplessness, memory loss.
And bad headaches. Says Robert Chan, Lee's best friend in
Hong Kong since his teen years, 'We all sensed something was
wrong, but we didn't pay attention to it. We thought it would
pass.'

Ever since moving to Hong Kong, Lee had sent regular
reports of his astounding successes to his former student, Ted
Ashley, at Warner Brothers. Producer Fred Weintraub flew to
Hong Kong to meet Lee on the set of *Game of Death*. In the
fall of 1972, Lee and Weintraub signed contracts. Bruce Lee
would get that for which he had striven for so long: he would
make his first film for international audiences and would
become a global star.

The proposed title of the picture was *Blood and Steel*,
which Lee fought hard with Ashley to change to *Enter the
Dragon* to signify his arrival. He stopped work on *Game of
Death* to begin production on *Enter the Dragon*.

'I feel this power bubbling up inside me,' he said. It is this
power – a beautiful lunacy – that we see roll off of Lee in his
movie fights. In *Enter the Dragon*, even when he stands still,
there's something inside him that vibrates; something
continues to move.

'Intense is the first word that comes to mind,' *Enter the
Dragon* co-producer Paul Heller says when asked to describe
Lee. 'He could focus himself at any one thing more totally
than anybody.'

Intense. Alive. During the filming of *Enter the Dragon*, Lee
supposedly told director Robert Clouse's wife that he would

die before his next birthday. At thirty-two. A year younger than Jesus.

Principal photography for *Enter the Dragon* was completed in April 1973. Lee edited fight scenes, dubbed his voice to the soundtrack, and went back to work on developing ideas for *Game of Death*. He had become regarded as a mystically empowered fighter and was regularly challenged through the press by would-be usurpers.

The tales of these 'duels' are no less mythological than the theories about his death. Popular legend has it that as a guest on *Enjoy Yourself Tonight*, Lee was challenged to push an older gung fu master out of his strongest fighting stance. Lee supposedly rose from his seat, sauntered across the stage and punched the old man in the face; according to the story, the master was knocked flat. 'I don't push,' Lee reportedly said by way of explanation. 'I punch.'

The source of this less than truthful legend: Lee himself, inventing the story for his students in the States. In both 1971 and 1972, in articles published in Hong Kong magazines, the 'I'm above competition' god of gung fu said that he'd thrown away all the trophies and plaques he'd won in America. 'Those things are empty, meaningless,' he said. 'They don't mean anything to me.' Lee had never entered a competition in America. Among other fictions in Golden Harvest press releases about Lee – he had earned a master's degree in philosophy from the University of Washington.

'It was like *Gunfight at the OK Corral*,' claims Heller of Lee's encounters in Hong Kong. 'They stand and tap their foot and you've got to take up the challenge. And Bruce would ignore it or walk away. Sometimes he couldn't. These were fierce encounters and the guys would get hurt. Bruce was so fast – he had reflexes and timing I defy anybody to this day to match.'

Mist and dreams. Although most tales of Lee's battles have no substance, it is true that newspaper ads offered movie contracts to the challenger who could dethrone the seemingly invincible Bruce Lee. He was the only star in the world who was coveted by studios everywhere: Warner Brothers, which had shunned him less than eighteen months before, hoped to sign him for several films, as did Carlo Ponti in Italy, as well as Taiwanese and other Hong Kong movie-makers.

On 10 May, while at Golden Harvest dubbing his voice for *Enter the Dragon*, Lee collapsed and was rushed to hospital, near death. He suffered a series of violent convulsions and an oedema of the brain. A neurologist administered a drug to reduce cerebral swelling and two and a half hours later, Lee became semi-conscious. It would be the next day before he could speak clearly.

The first week of June, the worried Lee flew to UCLA for further testing. His mother and brother now lived in LA. Upon receiving a clean bill of health, he stopped by the apartment that they shared. 'He was wondering how much he could push his body,' says younger brother Robert. 'He was constantly pushing himself to higher levels. He was always out to find more knowledge. He said, "Oh, man, the doctor told me I got a body like an eighteen-year-old." And he was thin but he was in good spirits.'

Lee also spoke with James Coburn. '"They told me I was in perfect shape, everything is cool. Just take it easy. Just take it easy for a while,"' Coburn quotes Lee as saying.

Six weeks later, on 20 July 1973, less than three weeks before the release of *Enter the Dragon*, Bruce Lee died.

Within hours, Linda Lee issued a statement saying that her husband had inexplicably collapsed while taking a walk with her in the meditation garden outside their home. Five days later, 25,000 people attended the funeral, the largest in the colony's history. Lee's body was flown to the US, where he was quietly buried in Seattle.

Enter the Dragon was released the second week of August. On the basis of that one picture, Bruce Lee became a worldwide celebrity. Japanese teenagers cut their hair like his. Hong Kong residents eulogised him as 'Three Legs Lee', a reference to his kicking ability, as well as his supposed sexual prowess. A cinema in Iran played *Enter the Dragon* daily from autumn 1973 until January 1979, when Shah Pahlavi was overthrown by the Ayatollah Khomeni. The chief lyrics and title of a hit disco song in India was 'Here's to That Swell Guy, Bruce Lee'. Over the years, millions of people came to see Lee's fight scenes as virtual religious artefacts.

'Everywhere I went,' says George Tan, 'the reaction was the same. I saw *Enter the Dragon* in Greece, France, New York, Hong Kong, London, Taiwan, the Philippines. Audiences everywhere related to Bruce Lee in primal ways. In death, it made him the first international man. It made everywhere I travelled home. Strange but true, *Enter the Dragon* made me a citizen of the world.'

Internationally, *Enter the Dragon* was Warner Brothers' highest grossing picture of 1973. By 1977, it was listed as one of the forty most profitable movies ever. It was re-released several times in the US; each time, it landed among the top five grossing pictures of the week. In the late seventies, inner-city drug dealers and pimps turned out for the picture with a similar reverence to Catholics attending mass. As of 20 July 1993, including video and television sales, *Enter the Dragon* had grossed over $300 million.

On the day of Lee's Hong Kong funeral, a newspaper disclosed that he had died, not with his wife, but in the apartment of the popular actress Betty Ting Pei, with whom he'd been having an affair.

At a quickly arranged inquest, Ting Pei testified that when Lee came to her apartment, he complained of a headache and she gave him a pill called Equagesic, the chief ingredients of which are aspirin and a common anti-anxiety agent. Lee went to lie on her bed and seemed to fall into a sleep from which he couldn't be roused. A professor of forensic medicine, R.D. Teare, flown from London for the case, determined the immediate cause of death to be cerebral oedema: Lee's brain had become swollen and had pressed violently against the inside of his skull. Among other findings: Lee had eaten hashish not only on the day of his death, but shortly before his 10 May collapse. Teare said that although there was no evidence that Lee had been murdered, his death appeared *not* to be from natural causes. Teare and the inquest jury concluded that oedema was caused by hypersensitivity to one or more of the ingredients in Equagesic. Bruce Lee had died not 'accidentally' but by 'misadventure'.

Before and during the inquest, Hong Kong papers devoted a riotous level of attention to rumours surrounding Lee's demise. Among the most popular theories: that he had died from overtraining or from too much sex, that he was murdered by angry gung fu masters, by the Chinese 'mafia'; that he was poisoned by a herbalist; that he was killed by a secret, invisible society of Ninja assassins (finally we know what happened in Dallas on 22 November 1963), by the director of his first two movies (less than three weeks before Lee's death, in an encounter widely reported in Hong Kong newspapers, he had threatened this director with a knife hidden in his belt buckle), by the head of Golden Harvest (who over the next twenty years would reap hundreds of millions of dollars from Lee's legend), by his lover(s), by his wife. Or that he simply had a congenital defect that was triggered by cannabis, by the intensity with which he lived, and/or by other non-murderous agents. Or, maybe most likely, from hypersensitivity not to an ingredient or ingredients in Equagesic but to cannabis, or a cannabis by-product.

'In my opinion,' says Dr Donald Langford, Lee's personal physician in Hong Kong and a former Baptist missionary, 'the same series of events that took place on May 10 is what killed Bruce Lee in July. Bruce was particularly sensitive to one or more of the alkaloids in cannabis. After the May incident, he was warned to stop eating the stuff, but he didn't listen. Every time I saw him, he was further and further into his own hype. Bruce's was a self-inflicted, though innocent, fatal illness.'

In the years following Lee's death, his reputation as a

martial artist became soiled not only by Chopalong Wong imitators (many people believe that Bruce Li is Bruce Lee and that Lee made dozens of movies), but by his own students. In 1972, Lee had closed his Los Angeles, Seattle and Oakland schools and demanded that his art not be taught. George Tan explains Lee's motives. 'He felt no one was qualified. This is a guy who was developing a reputation as the baddest man alive. He knew that the lack of quality in his students and teaching could come back to haunt him.'

With Lee's death and the unexpected success of *Enter the Dragon*, former students, most of whom had honest intentions of perpetuating Lee's teaching methods, also recognised that considerable money could be made by claiming to be heirs to his art. Says Tan: 'Bruce knew that this would happen. It's like Christianity or most any other thing. First, along comes an innovator. He dies and the guys left behind are followers. Most of them don't have a clue what Bruce was saying or doing, let alone ability to execute it.'

Over the past three decades, jeet kune do has become much of what Lee sought to change in the martial arts: it is structured, systematic, unintentionally worshipful, dogmatic. 'If Bruce knew what some of these guys were teaching and calling JKD,' says former Lee student and world heavyweight kick-boxing champion, Joe Lewis, 'he'd claw his way out of his grave and kick their shiny behinds.'

On 31 March 1993, near the twentieth anniversary of Lee's death, his only son, Brandon Bruce Lee, was accidentally killed on a movie set in Wilmington, North Carolina. The younger Lee was shot by a round fired from a .44-calibre handgun that was supposed to have contained blanks. It was the first time in the history of film that an actor, much less the leading man, had been shot and killed on the set.

Brandon Lee had admired his father and had difficulty separating the myths he'd heard from the breathing human being he had known only briefly. He said he wept when he saw Bruce Lee posters hanging in martial arts academies and was often challenged by schoolmates who had heard that he was the son of Bruce Lee. Brandon Lee had not wanted to be a martial artist or to make action movies. He studied drama at Emerson College in Boston and took acting lessons in Manhattan in the hope of becoming a serious actor, but had little success getting the roles he wanted and eventually chose to take advantage of his unique heritage. He decided to jump-start his career by making a few martial arts movies and believed he would then effect the transition to more serious movie-making.

By the spring of 1993, Brandon Lee had starred in two movies for American producers and had recently made multiple-picture deals with 20th Century-Fox and with Carolco Studios. In his first feature for Carolco, *The Crow*, Brandon's role was that of a pop idol who has been resurrected from the dead to avenge his own murder. Principal photography was almost completed. The scene being filmed when he was shot was one in which his character is killed. It's not a dissimilar plot to many of the exploitation films about his father.

Legendary rumours about the father's death seemed ready-prepared for the son's. It was as if Louis B. Mayer had won the heavenly game show, *God for a Day*, and had chosen to publicise the May release of *Dragon: The Bruce Lee Story*. The seeming synchronicity between the deaths of Bruce and Brandon Lee caused even greater confusion about the elder Lee's exit; details became blurred, intertwined. Many people came to remember Bruce Lee as having been shot and murdered. Within weeks of Brandon Lee's death, the son's story had become a footnote to the father's legend.

On 28 April 1993, at a ceremony during which Bruce Lee received a star on the Hollywood Walk of Fame (no real recognition for Lee, but a studio manoeuvre to promote *Dragon*), Linda Lee spoke of her son less than a month after his death. 'If Bruce were here today, he would want to say to the film community that "this must never happen again". And so I am calling for a positive call to action to the film community . . . to take measures that the safety precautions that they have on their film sets will never lead to this series of negligent acts that took the life of my son . . . We expect that a young life will not be wasted in vain.'

To me, what is most notable about the well-intentioned widow's and mother's use of language is that she's tortured by the effort to sound literate, to be profound and empowered. She is the star of a 1960s Massengill commercial, running through a field of daisies in a plastic dress. She becomes, in effect, an emissary for, and agent of, the very machine she's trying to evangelise against. The effect is no call for change but a studio stunt to promote *Dragon* not as the piece of pulp fiction it is but as *the* authentic Bruce Lee film biography.

So. Before Bruce Lee's name is enveloped further by the deifying mists of pop mythology, perhaps it would be useful to define what the person who breathed and dreamed and died has left us. For what accomplishments has Lee not been properly credited?

He revolutionised Asian fighting disciplines, made them organically American and evangelised this product around the globe. In the 1960s, there were less than five hundred martial arts schools in the world; by the early 1990s, because of his influence, there were more than ten million martial arts students in the US alone. 'There isn't a martial artist on the planet who hasn't been influenced by Bruce Lee,' says Tan. 'This doesn't mean that most are better fighters than they were before Bruce came along. It just means they picked up some of his concepts or methods.'

In addition, Lee fundamentally changed movie fight scenes: those of us born before 1960 grew up in a culture that considered kicking to be 'dirty' fighting; martial arts are now employed in nearly every fight in every action movie. And, of course, we can learn much about late twentieth-century marketing, and even more interestingly, the manner in which religions have been created throughout the centuries, by observing the Bruce Lee legend machine.

There is, after all, another Lee legacy: those who are looking for the way, the truth and the life through Lee and who don't recognise that, if there is such a thing as wisdom, it probably won't be found in a guy who wants to be a movie star. These are the most rabid of fans, the ones such as Andy Nocktagal, who moved to a motel in Seattle near Lee's gravesite. Nocktagal changed his name to Dalton Lee (the name of the Patrick Swayze character in *Roadhouse*) and claims to be the son of Bruce Lee and Lindsay *Bionic Woman* Wagner. And there's Mikey Miyazaki, the son of a wealthy Tokyo businessman who made his bedroom into a composite of the sets Lee used in *Enter the Dragon*. TV monitors were mounted to the ceiling in the corners and he perpetually played a different Lee movie on all four monitors. Then there's Blaze Leung, who lives in LA, claims that he is Bruce Lee and has his wife dress like Linda Lee and cut her hair in the beehive style that Lee's wife wore in the sixties. At sunset each evening for more than a decade, yet another true believer takes a Bruce Lee shrine to a beach near Venice, California, and says prayers. And there's retired Mongolian physician, Ichinorov Dendev, who, in the spring of 1993, set off on a nine-month sojourn, during which he and two 'black belt jeet kune do' disciples 'walked' across the Bering Straits on the way from Mongolia to Seattle (reportedly wearing out five pairs of shoes each) to place flowers on the grave of the god of martial arts. And in the early eighties a young Londoner hijacked a bus and rammed it through a shopfront screaming, 'I'm Bruce Lee, I'm God. I'm Bruce Lee, I'm God.'

Most significantly among Lee-ites, however, is the case of John Little, a former writer for a bodybuilding magazine who, in the 1990s, after the birth of a son he named Brandon, moved from his home in Canada to a house on the same block as Linda Lee-Cadwell's residence in Meridian, Idaho. The former spouse of the king of gung fu had married an attorney named Bruce and, arguably for the first time ever, was living her own life. (It's fair to say that Bruce Lee's relationship with his timid wife was oppressive. Linda Lee was, in many ways, rescued by the death of 'Small Dragon Lee'.)

John Little's mission was to become the official/unofficial voice of the Nation of Lee-ism and, in this, he pretty much succeeded, negotiating permission from Lee's widow to compile and publish Lee's handwritten journals – not original work, but notes that Lee had copied almost word-for-word from the writings of Jiddu Krishnamurti, Alan Watts, Fritz Perls, Eric Hoffer, Carl Rogers, Mao Tse Tung, even Benjamin Franklin; from classic Chinese literature, old boxing and wrestling texts, and from quotes by Jack Dempsey, Rocky Marciano, Gene Tunney, 'Sugar' Ray Robinson and a host of others. 'Bruce Lee had ability to recognise key insights in other people's work,' explains George Tan. 'But he couldn't have written them himself – and, as far as we know, he didn't claim to. Those claims came after he was dead and gone.' In a ten-volume series with such ridiculous titles as *Bruce Lee: Artist of Life*, *Bruce Lee: Words from a Master* and *Striking Thoughts: Bruce Lee's Wisdom for Daily Living* (books that feature such equally ludicrous chapter headings as, on nutrition, 'Fuelling the Dragon' and 'Enter the [vitamin] Supplements'), Tuttle Publishing and Contemporary Books published Lee's and Little's tracings (for which Little was paid many tens of thousands of dollars) – without attributing quotes to the actual authors (including lines Little stole from *Enter the Dragon* and from the 1971 television series *Longstreet*, on which Lee guest-starred as a philosophical martial arts teacher) – as, in Little's words, 'entirely the achievement' of Bruce Lee, who Little referred to as 'one of the most intelligent philosophical minds of the twentieth century'.

Interviewed for TV documentaries, Little spoke of Lee in the first person and present tense – as if his old friend Bruce just happened to be sitting with his arm draped across Little's shoulders – and was billed as Lee's 'friend and historian' (they never met), and in a martial arts magazine said that he had been 'chosen' (as in mystically empowered) to deliver the king of movie gung fu's gospel to the world. Little's closest thing to a piece of original work about Lee is a largely plagiarised book, 'co-written' with Ms Lee-Cadwell, published with the fully fatuous title, *The Warrior Within: The Philosophies of Bruce Lee to Better Understand the World Around You and Achieve a Rewarding Life*. Describing Lee for this volume, Little writes, 'How could a man who only lived thirty-two years have been so deep, so insightful, and also such a prolific writer, a loyal friend, an attentive father, a devoted husband, a dedicated artist and self-help authority?' Among Little's most visible accomplishments is a schlockumentary in which he sewed together remnants from Lee's unfinished *Game of Death*. On these decades-old, badly edited fight scenes for which sound had never been recorded, Little dubbed his own voice as that of Lee, not only for the scant dialogue Lee 'spoke', but for his chicken-in-mensa battle screams.

So. What is the value in getting Bruce Lee's story right?

What reason is there to dispel a few legends and for the first time publicly arrive at some kind of truth?

After all, even Lee's most 'important' accomplishment (being driven to try to punch and kick people better than anyone in the history of the world) is certainly less than ennobling.

Other American tales are remembered – James Dean, Scott and Zelda Fitzgerald, Marilyn, the Kennedys: those doomed dreamers (and purveyors) of the dream. And Greeks are recalled: Sisyphus, Narcissus, Icarus.

What's different about Lee? That he appeared to be so conscious, so awake, so in control? That he was a 'master'? That he seemed downright invulnerable?

Perhaps the most resonant (and even most accurate) mythology is that Lee was murdered by his own myopic ambition, by his arrogance in believing that he could create himself.

'I use no way as way, have no limitation as limitation,' claimed Bruce Lee. I can't think of a more poignant epitaph for the self-obsessed twentieth-century.

PART THREE:
PERSONAL BATTLES

AMERICAN VIDEO

Triad Style, 13 July 1997.

This was my first piece of published fiction. As an adult, I've been intrigued by women who, in one way or another, are not classically feminine, who are cocky enough to believe, no matter how naively, that they wind and set their own clocks. The not-always-likeable protagonist in this story, Kat, is based on several people: on Susan Foster May, an employee and friend when I managed video shops in North Carolina; on my former wife Lyn; on my friend, women's world featherweight kick-boxing champion Kathy Long; and on my own aching dreaminess as I struggled to teach myself to write during my late adolescence and then throughout the eight years I felt trapped in my job as a retail video manager.

I began 'American Video' in 1986, under the title 'Kat and the Movies', when Lyn and I were living near Louisville, Kentucky. (I remember the evening the story started taking shape. We were walking beside the Ohio River when we both noticed the black silhouette of an airliner pass through the middle of a recently risen orange moon.) Four years later, between non-fiction sports magazine assignments that I didn't feel particularly challenged by or interested in, I found 'American Video' in a desk drawer and rewrote it in the house we'd recently bought in Winston-Salem, North Carolina, patterning it partly after several Tobias Wolff stories. My studio was in the attic; when I was home alone, I'd often open the windows at the rear of the house and climb out and sit on the roof, watching, listening to and feeling the neighbourhood below and around me. All during the weeks that I worked on this story, and now every time that I read it, I see a composite of both of these neighbourhoods that Lyn and I lived in – our rooftops, our neighbours – as well as the house I grew up in, my father's home, and finally my grandparents' house, where our then seven-year-old daughter Johanna kissed a pane of glass on an outside door leaving her lip imprints behind (another real-life instance I borrowed for 'American Video'). Characters' names throughout the story are those of people Lyn and I knew, though most of the people don't resemble those characters. I also wrote my dog Dallas into the story. He was my friend: he deserves any sort of continuance – or illusion of continuance – that I might help him find.

Other than 'American Video', all the pieces in this final section can accurately be called memoir.

1

Kat looked at the clock. It was almost five. She'd been alone since she came in at three. It was seventy-five degrees and new leaves on maples in the parking lot looked wet with sun. Mr Simons had said that spring was the worst time of year for business. Kat was glad. Although she couldn't get away with sitting outside and soaking up the rays, she'd propped open the front door trying to feel a breeze.

She could hear the couple coming from all the way across the parking lot. They had to be married, she was sure; otherwise they wouldn't argue so much in public. These two were so bad that Kat couldn't help but stop her work and watch. They just wouldn't let up, especially the man, who was wearing round, mirrored sunglasses and olive work clothes and who was short and thick and mean-looking. Whenever the woman got off a good line, he tightened his mouth, his lips went pale and he shook his head from side to side. The man noticed that Kat was watching. He pulled off his glasses and stared at her. In the bald spring light, pock-marks in his cheeks looked dark and deep.

Kat wanted to kick this creep in his jewels. After she graduated, when she became a kick-boxing champ, she'd come back to this shitty little town and do just that. She wanted to remember exactly what this dickface looked like. He had deep-set yellowed eyes; his hair was black and combed straight back and was as shiny as feathers on a big fat crow.

'It's their problem, not ours,' the man was saying. 'Leave the goddamn thing and let's go.'

The woman seemed not to pay attention. She stepped to the counter and tugged a cassette from its case. 'There's a problem with this tape,' she said.

The man set his jaw and said, 'You're just goddamn askin' for it, aren't you,' then turned his back. Kat watched him light a cigarette beside the big red NO SMOKING sign then stride from the store. He walked across the lot. As he got in on the passenger's side of a little once-had-been-silver Chevy, the door hinges made a loud popping noise. He left the door open and one brown boot on the pavement.

Kat looked at the wife. The woman's eyes were red and they bulged, as if her husband had grabbed her around the neck and had squeezed, not real hard, but very steadily, for many, many years. Marriages were like this most of the time, Kat knew. She could still see her own father standing over her mother at the kitchen table, talking down at Mom like she was a tapeworm or something. And Kat could see her mother's face go all ancient-ugly when her father treated her that way and Mom would stand up and get a few inches away from Dad and yell and call him all kinds of names while his face went sort of blank and he stared off kind of calm and empty-eyed.

And Kat knew that she would always remember the

Thursday afternoon that everything changed. When none of this between her mother and father would ever happen again. And how she and Todd were right there in the kitchen when Dad came in from work and it all just sort of happened, just tumbled out right in front of them. And then they had to sell the house and Dad was living out West somewhere with somebody called Carol, or maybe Carolyn. Or was it Karen? Kat couldn't be certain.

Now, in the store, Kat was sure the customer hadn't been crying; she was a regular and Kat was certain her eyes always looked this way.

'Try it in your machine,' she told Kat. 'I want to see what it does for you. He said not to tell you about it. But it's my responsibility to let you know.'

Kat popped the tape into the VCR under the counter, pushed play and returned to checking in new movies. 'It got to this point and we couldn't make it go no more,' explained the customer. 'He said it's their problem, take the tape back. They can find it themselves, he said. But I spend a lot of money and time in here, it's the only place I use, and I said if I don't tell them they'll never know. It'll get put back up on the shelf. And I'd be exactly like all the other jerks . . . See, there it goes!' she said, pointing excitedly at the TV as an angry face with a long knife disappeared from the screen. 'That's exactly what it did in our machine. He said not to tell you about it. He gets me so flustrated sometimes.'

To Kat, the customer looked like *she'd* been stabbed, though Kat didn't show any kind of reaction and hardly looked up from her work. 'I'm sorry you had a problem,' she finally said, not sounding sorry at all. 'Why don't you pick out another movie.'

'Free of charge?' the customer asked.

Kat didn't look at the customer, but nodded.

'That's why I keep coming here,' the customer said. She was smiling. 'You're such nice people. You always take care of my problems.'

Kat watched the customer walk away from the counter. 'Fat people shouldn't wear warm-up suits,' she said under her breath, and went back to checking in new rental tapes.

The title she was working on was *Revenge of the Samurai Sluts from Hell*. Mr Simons had bought five copies. A title like that just had to be a good renter. She was entering the tapes into the computer's inventory when the customer came back to the counter. The woman didn't have any rental movies with her; she had pulled three tapes from the sales bin.

'I need to see your membership card and drivers' licence,' Kat said.

'I just want to know if you can hold these till I get paid,' the customer said. 'About three weeks. And there's somethin' else I need to know – Can I get a card in my name? Just my name. Not his.' With her head, she motioned toward the parking lot.

'You'll need to fill out a membership application,' Kat said.

The woman looked at the man. His foot was still sticking out of the car door. 'He won't stay here that long. Just want to be sure I can get a card myself. Don't think I could do without this place.'

She pulled a wallet from her purse and opened it. Tucked in the scratched plastic sleeve was a picture of two tight-faced, light-haired boys in suits and white shirts with collars that looked like they dug into their necks. 'I'm always buying movies. He likes to rent – I buy.' She flipped through receipts in her chequebook. 'Here's one for $41.58 made to American Video, another for $90.37, one for $26.35 . . . and here's one for $139.81 – that's when I got my tax money back.'

'That's a lot of money for movies,' Kat said.

The woman laughed a tired laugh. 'He doesn't like me spending so much. But at least the movies are mine, if nothing else is, that's the way I look at it. I just got to be sure I can have my own card – you're sure it won't be a problem, now? I've got to know. Tonight, before we got here, we had a big set-to over that tape he rented. And I need to know, when we split . . . if I leave tomorrow, that I'll be able to get my own card.'

'People break up all the time and need their own memberships,' Kat said.

The customer nodded. The corners of her eyes were wet, but her voice did not shake and her eyes did not get more red than they already had been. She walked from the store, opened the door on the driver's side of the car, and squeezed slowly in behind the wheel. The car sank noticeably and seemed to sigh. Her husband swung his foot up, it disappeared inside the car, he popped his door closed.

A tall man jogged past the door. 'Guys with skinny legs shouldn't wear shorts,' Kat said.

She kept staring outside. Shadows from trees were sharp and precise, leaves coin-bright, daffodil blossoms almost blinding. She wanted to climb the biggest oak she could find and sit in the sun all the way at the top, where she could gain an unobstructed view of sky. She wasn't scared of heights. She wanted to string a line to the next big oak fifty feet away and walk barefoot from one tree to the next. She was certain she'd do something like this when she became a high-wire artist.

Kat looked at the clock on the wall under the row of TVs. It was 5.19. When she'd come to work, she'd decided she didn't want to answer the phone today; she had unplugged it. Now she hooked it up, turned off the stereo, and slid a copy of *E.T.* into the VCR. Mr Simons might come in early and it'd be best if she looked like she was ready to do business and if she was playing something he'd call 'a family film'.

The phone hadn't been on the hook two minutes before it rang. 'Kathleen,' her mother said, 'who've you been talking to all afternoon?' Mom was calling from the phone in the hall beside the bathroom. Kat heard the shower running in the background.

'Nobody,' Kat answered. 'We've been busy.' She heard a deep, slow-talking man's voice. When it stopped, there were violins and then there were horns. 'Are you getting ready to go out, Mom?' Kat asked.

Her mother didn't answer.

'Are you wanting me to watch Todd again tonight, Mother?'

'I may go out for a while,' her mother said. 'You don't mind do you, baby?'

Kat curled her top lip and closed her eyes. When she realised she'd made a face, she felt guilty, embarrassed. But why should I? she thought, and made the face again.

'Sugar, you get off at seven, don't you? Why don't you walk down to the post office and catch the bus. I won't be gone but just a little while.'

Kat heard another man's voice singing. Was that Frank Sinatra, or Elvis, or Wayne Newton, or Garth Brooks, or who? It didn't matter. She knew it was some greasy old fart. Why did Mom always listen to this Vegasy crap when she was getting ready to go out? Mom ate right and worked out all the time and was taking English classes over at Davidson Community College and was way too smart to listen to something that made her seem so dumb. Kat couldn't understand.

'OK, Mom, I'll ride the bus.'

'Fix yourself something good to eat, honey. And see to it that Todd gets in bed by 9.30. Don't you have a spelling test tomorrow? You be sure to study for it.'

Then her mother hung up and there was no music on the other end of the line.

It was eight minutes before six. Kat's work was almost done, including getting the new movies ready for rent. All that was left was to put them on the shelves. Then she'd have a couple of minutes to take it easy. She saw the scissors, the tape, the fat felt-tipped markers, the inventory pages she'd left on the counter. Mr Simons could clean them up. He needed to do something to earn the megabucks he was paid. There were still no customers in the store.

'*Revenge of the Samurai Sluts from Hell*,' Kat said aloud, looking at the title once again. She remembered Mr Simons staring at the picture of the girls on the cover when he was making his order, staring at their long pink tongues all stuck out toward each other with little white bumps on them and their inflated suntanned mammaries thrust up high. And not a sword or a samurai outfit anywhere. 'Jesus, this'll rent,' he'd said, but not exactly to Kat, who was standing behind him. Or to anyone.

Now Kat couldn't help but laugh. Men could really be stupid. Sometimes they didn't even know when they were being made fun of. '*Samurai Sluts from Hell*.' Cripes, what a title. She picked up two copies of the movie, one in each hand, and felt their weight. What is it they see in this stuff? she wondered. What is it that they get out of it? Or what is it somebody wants that he's not going to find when he opens the box?

She remembered the time she'd walked up on Todd down by the creek. She was standing above him beside the white pines. He was looking at the magazine on the ground and he held his thing in his hands and was yanking real fast until it shot out over the water what must've been a couple yards. The little turd had set some kind of world record, she was sure. She remembered the fresh smell of pines and the cold, creepy one of damp ground and how disappointed Todd had looked from behind as he zipped up his jeans. You could see the sadness in his shoulders.

Now she thought a moment, then smiled the same smile she practised when taking off her clothes at night in her bedroom mirror. She laid both tapes on the counter and went and grabbed her purse from under the stool beside the phone. She pulled something from inside and turned her back to the door, concealing what she was doing, although she knew no one was there to watch. When she stepped back to the front counter, she carefully snapped open the first case, then the second, and slowly, ritualistically, brought both open boxes to face level. She opened her mouth until it formed a circle.

124

She wanted to laugh but didn't. She knew she looked ready to give, pleased to receive. She placed a soft wet kiss on the dark inside of each case. Before closing the boxes and shelving the cassettes, she checked to see that the shining pink lip imprints she had left were perfect.

2

Kat couldn't keep her eyes off the clock. It was almost eight. Mr Simons had never been this late. Geez, didn't he know other people had lives? Kat had a good mind to just walk out and leave the door standing open. I would, too, she thought, if I didn't need money to go to the beach. And for kick-boxing class. She couldn't wait until she got to be famous so she wouldn't have to put up with any of this any more. She'd buy herself a horse ranch and ride through sweet-smelling woods and shining green meadows all day long.

The store had been busy for over an hour. The biggest lines came around 6.30, when the thunderstorm rolled in, and ever since it had been too busy to call Mr Simons. Movies that Kat hadn't been able to get checked in were stacked ten high all over the counters. People were scavenging through the coloured cases, tossing blue and red and tan and green rectangles all over the place like some kind of adult's Erector set and making even bigger messes.

While bagging a couple silly old musicals for slow old Mrs Beeson, Kat took a quick reading on the computer. It said she'd done about $300 since seven. At $1.49 per tape that was a lot of people. Too many damn people. Maybe a half-hour ago, a good-looking dark-haired guy had been standing at the end of the counter, trying to find the time and nerve, she was sure, to ask for her number. Shit. She couldn't even make the chance to say more than 'hi' to him. After about fifteen minutes, she looked up and he was gone. And, oh God, she now realised, I missed the last bus at 7.45. I hope it's not too late to call Mom.

She left the counter without excusing herself and she picked up the phone. She looked at her feet as she dialled, not wanting to see people rolling their eyes or shuffling all around. She let it ring ten times. No answer. Damn, hell and piss. Well, at least she must've taken Todd with her.

Kat hung up the phone just as Mr Simons moved behind the counter. He was carrying his shoulders kind of low, his arms at his sides; his hands were dark pink and splotched, his hair and forehead were damp and sticky-looking with sweat. 'Don't say anything,' he said. 'I'm sorry I'm late. Don't be hard on me. We've all got it tough sometimes.'

He was wearing a pair of wrinkled khakis, a starched white shirt and a loose-fitting blue blazer with a big yellow patch sewn on it that read BERT'S SAVS MOR. Kat hadn't known until that moment that managing American Video was Mr Simons's second job.

'You put up movies, I'll wait on people,' he told Kat. 'I appreciate you being here,' he said, trying to smile. He stepped to the second terminal and said, 'I can help someone down here.'

3

When Kat pulled in the driveway, the only light in the house was the muted glow from Todd's night light. She stopped near the garage, switched off the ignition and removed the keys, but when she got out of Mr Simons's old orange Toyota, it was making a chugging noise and was spewing shining blue smoke into the night, which it continued to do as she unlocked the door to the house.

'Take my car,' Mr Simons had said when Kat told him she didn't have a ride. 'I'll have the wife pick me up.' Although Kat was too young to get a licence, Mr Simons didn't know it. She looked old for her age and to get the job she had lied and said she was seventeen. Kat was an experienced driver.

Now she squeaked the screen closed behind her and

stepped carefully through the dark. She liked walking in these black rooms. She wasn't afraid and she enjoyed feeling the familiar shapes around her.

She opened the refrigerator, grabbed a soda and an open bag of chips lying on the counter and she walked, through the dark, toward the light in Todd's room. She smelled the smell from halfway down the hall. It made her not want to eat and she left the bag of chips on the phone table outside the room. It was a warm, too-sweet odour, the smell of an old movie theatre. She looked at her brother from the doorway. He was lying on his back, mouth open a full inch and red hair jutting out from his head at unrelated angles. Kat frowned at her brother, thinking he looked even uglier in his sleep than when he was awake. She put her soda on his nightstand and took a seat at the foot of his bed. The sheet of plastic on the mattress made a crinkling sound. Almost twelve years old and still wetting the bed. She felt embarrassed by him and couldn't see how he wasn't ashamed just to be alive.

She reached under the covers. At least they're not wet tonight. She pulled at Todd's closest foot and brought it out into the dim light. She grabbed his big toe and held it above the bed a few inches until be began to kick in his sleep. Then she dropped the foot and Todd rubbed his eyes and squinted.

'Where's Mom?' Kat asked.

'You know what, Kathy?' Todd said.

'No, I don't,' she said, and made a face. 'Don't call me Kathy,' she said. 'Where's Mom? She's supposed to be home by now.'

'Kathy, you don't ever listen to me. I'm trying to tell you something. Guess what happened today? – I was outside throwing the Frisbee to Dallas. We were just playing Frisbee and he wasn't bothering nobody. Then Quinn came over and asked if he could throw the Frisbee, too. I said no, but he kept begging. So I let him and he turned around and threw it up on the roof and he laughed and ran away.'

'Where's Mom, Todd?'

'Geez, Kat, I don't know. Will you just listen to me? I'm trying to tell you something. Dallas wouldn't leave the yard. He kept running back and forth, looking up at the roof and me and running and barking and whining and stuff, and just hanging around and looking up at the roof and whining and barking until he made himself plumb sick. Then Mom came out and got him and kicked him in the head and shut him up in the basement.'

'Where's Mom now?' Kat said.

Todd sighed and shrugged and rocked his head back and forth. 'I don't know. Maybe down at the bar or over at Liz's or with Uncle Larry or Uncle Eddie or somebody. She said she wouldn't be long.'

Kat kicked the side of Todd's bed for no reason, then walked to the bathroom. She washed her face and hands, and before leaving the room, threw several hard punches at the mirror over the sink and thrust her hands over her head in a sign of victory.

She cracked open the basement door and in the slice of light that spilled down the stairs, she saw Dallas asleep at the bottom of the steps. He was lying on his side with his tail tucked under his body and his legs stiff out in front of him. He was breathing quickly, shallowly, and his feet were making small running movements and the flap of skin over his mouth was puffing out and he was making little barking sounds.

'Stupid-ass dog,' she said, and closed the door. 'Somebody should shoot his ass.'

In the kitchen, Kat reached into the refrigerator, past the orange juice and the container of non-fat cottage cheese, past the grapefruits and the bag of Golden Delicious apples, and she snapped one of her mother's cans of Budweiser from a six-pack. She went to the back door. She opened the screen and leaned against the frame, staring past her boss's now silent car and out across the yard, not seeing anything, but listening to the sounds of a party over at the condos. She heard men laughing. She imagined the laughing men to be muscular yet sophisticated, like the ones in some music videos and in magazine ads, like ones she'd have when she made her own videos. They wouldn't be tired and fat and hairy and crude or drive old Toyotas or Chevys or watch movies about samurai sluts. They were from Manhattan and Paris and Hollywood and Zanzibar. She placed her hands on her hips and again smiled the hot yet cold smile she practised in her mirror. When standing in front of the mirror, she thought of herself as smiling for the camera that was always nearby, waiting to film the important parts of her life, all the moments that made her special.

She gently closed the screen behind her and opened the storage shed but didn't turn on the light. She placed the can of beer in the left pocket of her jeans skirt and turned to the side, where she could use her lead hand to carefully feel in front of her. *Ninjas learn to move beautifully at night*, she thought. Feeling her way around, she found the handlebars of her old Schwinn and remembered that the ladder had been stored behind the bike she used to ride. She reached across the Schwinn and felt the unmistakable, almost electric, feel of the aluminum shaft. She grabbed the big stepladder and hefted it over her bike. The back of the ladder caught the rear handlebar and, as the bike fell, it raked hard across her left shin.

'Oh, shit and piss,' she hissed through closed teeth, and after sitting the ladder on the floor, she hopped up and down to avoid making more noise and waking Mrs Parson next door. Every night, the old biddy went to bed when the sun went down. Kat left the Schwinn where it had fallen, but walked the ladder from the shed and opened it near the side of the house.

She took her can of beer and moved it to her right pocket, pulled her short skirt up on the left side and tied it in a knot at the waist. The ladder reached a little more than halfway up the wall. As she climbed, she felt blood run down her calf and into her shoe. Two steps from the top, she still wasn't close to where she needed to be. She moved to the last rung, and almost immediately placed one foot and then the other on top of the ladder, where there was a big sticker that read: DO NOT STAND HERE.

Kat's head finally cleared the roof, and she saw the Frisbee. It was three feet from the edge, glowing ghostlike under the moon. She reached over the gutter and laid hands and forearms across the cold, rough shingles that were still wet from the thunderstorm. Stretching, she could just manage to touch the Frisbee with the very tips of her fingers.

'A little more,' she said, standing on her toes and reaching across – reaching, reaching. 'Just a little more.' She could feel the jagged breaks in the plastic where the dog had bitten.

Kat's feet pushed against the ladder. And they pushed farther. And then the ladder tipped back and was gone. Kat reached for the gutter, it pulled away in her left hand. But she's quick and has great good luck; she grabs the edge of the roof with both hands and holds, fast, thinking, *I will not fall.* The ladder clunks to the ground; the gutter makes a hollow clanking/clattering sound as it hits. But no lights come on at Mrs Parson's.

Kat knows that what comes next will be hard. She rests a moment, thinking, *I will do this.* Then: she muscles herself up, using arms and shoulders. Less than halfway there, she reaches a sticking point and falls back. But Kat does two hundred push-ups a day; she is strong and determined. When she tries again, she forces her shuddering torso to get her where she needs to be. Her body does not fail, she's sure it will never fail. She straightens her elbows then locks them out, and she stops and rests again. When her strength returns, she swings a leg across and on to the roof. Now she flexes the muscles of her quadriceps and shoves as hard as she can off the ball of her foot; she finds she has the leverage that she requires. She makes it to the roof, exhausted, panting. She lies belly down with her eyes closed, feeling the hard rising roof against the jutting places on her hips, upper ribs, and pressing into her breasts. She concentrates on slowing her breath. Bits of black rock on the shingles bite into her cheek. She's grateful the shingles are there to hurt her.

Kat stays where she is, her eyes closed, feeling little rocks grind into her skin, until she stops shaking and her breath is calm and she no longer feels that she's going to puke. She blinks, breathes deep, opens her eyes, turns her head to the right and sees it again. The Frisbee. Glowing. Almost pulsing.

She reaches over, takes up the disc, feels its balance, holds it level. She slowly sits up and when she gets herself where she wants to be, she sails the Frisbee out across the fescue, watching the entire arc of its perfect smooth flight. The disc lands in the dead centre of Mrs Parson's new tomato plants.

Kat sits on the roof and studies her leg and the trail of blood that looks black in the night. She watches three guys play with a football out in the road under a street light in front of the Spinellis'. For guys, they're not making much noise. Kat wonders if they can see her. She sees somebody in the kitchen over at the Watsons', moving around behind the curtains. Mr Watson comes out the back door and on to his deck; he's holding a cup in his hand. He steps over to his Japanese maple. Although Kat can't see his face – he's too far away – she believes that he's smiling. She breathes a deep breath and looks at the clearing sky, noticing patterns among the stars: the Big Dipper's the only name she knows, but she sees other constellations. She watches the black silhouette of a distant airliner pass through the middle of the moon.

Soon, Kat will walk to the side of the house and jump the four feet down to the garage roof. From there, she'll leap to the ground, then land and roll and come up easy. She'll step to the side of the house, kick off both shoes, wash her wounded leg and elbows and knees with the hose, then run barefoot through wet shining grass to retrieve the Frisbee from Mrs Parson's tomatoes. Kat will take the toy in the house and lay it on the little table to the right of the door, where Dallas will see it when he's let out in the morning.

But now, before that happens, Kat will reach into her

pocket and pull out her beer. Droplets of water will slide down the can and refract the moon's light. She'll open the beer and smile slightly to herself at the little sweet explosion of effervescence. In the silence, the sound will be nearly as big as in the commercials.

Her first gulp of beer will be noisy and, upon swallowing, she'll make a pinched face, shaking her head from side to side, shivering. The second taste will be smaller and Kat will restrain from showing a reaction.

Kat will ache everywhere but, like other professionals, she'll be proud of the pain. In a way, it'll feel good. She's earned the pain, she's accomplished something, she owns the pain.

She knows how privileged she is tonight: to be sitting up here safe and strong, separate from the noise down below while believing she's closer to the wind and to the sky; to see the movement of people's lives without being bound by the details.

She'll draw a slow, slow, deep, deep breath and will quickly peel off her T-shirt. Her skin had been bristling with chill even before she'd removed the top. She'll flip her shirt into the air with the same controlled abandon cowgirls use when they throw their hats into the emptiness. She'll place her hands behind her head and stretch and relish the cold air and her own hair on her bare back and arms. And in April moonlight, Kat will glow with the certainty of her own invulnerability.

a secret

Triad Style, 4 November 1997.

I began working on this story in autumn 1981 after my wife Lyn had left me and moved back in with her parents, taking our infant daughter Johanna with her, chiefly because I had refused to get a full-time job while I was teaching myself to write. Before, when I had featured myself as a character in my stories, I had been a nearly superhuman adventurer. That changed when Lyn left me. Among many other things, I'm grateful to her for having been one of my best, and most grounding, editors.

THE CAROLINA THEATRE was the last of Winston-Salem's stately old movie palaces. Inside, it was adorned with ornate marble sconces, pseudo-Greek statues of gods, goddesses and heroes, and a dust-rich red velvet curtain that looked to weigh about a hundred tons.

On Saturday mornings at nine o'clock the velvet curtain rose and, for ten cents admission, children twelve and under were treated to a cartoon and a weekly episode of a *Rocket Man*, *Batman* or *Superman* serial; we played bingo for movie passes, popcorn, sodas and candy; and we were shown a full-length cowboy or monster picture. I was drawn to the mystery of the old Carolina, mesmerised by the power that oversized lighted screens and big hidden speakers have when placed at the front of large dark rooms.

On Friday and Saturday nights, Daddy would take my sister Carol and me to westerns or to Disneys. I remember a summer evening in 1964 when Carol was spending the night with a friend. I recall riding in the car with Daddy and stopping for a cone of soft-serve vanilla ice cream on the way to a double feature at the Winston-Salem Drive-In. And, as the ice cream dripped across my fingers, Daddy said, 'Need to tell you 'bout these movies, son.' His words, his tone and the look on his face were obviously intended to carry weight.

'You'll see some things with women you never seen,' he continued. I didn't understand what he meant, only that he sounded nervous, protective, and maybe a little guilty. 'Nothin' to get worked up about, Dave,' he assured me.

The movies that night were *Doctor No* and *Goldfinger*. Hours later, entirely worked up, I lay wide awake in bed, recalling not the women on the screen, but how James Bond had been so screw-everybody cool, and how he had disposed of all the bad guys, effortlessly and systematically, the power magically vested in him by late twentieth-century technology and by a strange, mystical Japanese science called 'karate.'

A few weeks later, Daddy told me about a new TV show, *The Man from U.N.C.L.E.* We watched the first episode together. And again, there they were, these secret agent types, these coolest of the cool. To me, the hero, Napoleon Solo, was badder than Bond, cooler than zero, as he righteously battled and almost effortlessly destroyed each and every foe, seldom, if ever, being hurt in return, having been rendered inde-structible (and incredibly cocky) by near-magical gadgetry, and by knowledge of that same exotic and miraculous 'karate'.

Over the next four years, I ached to become Agent Solo. Weekday afternoons until Daddy got home from work, I crept from room to room in the house, shooting evil counter-agents (who fell bloodlessly dead before my eyes) and delivering lethal karate chops a hair's breadth away from lamps, bedposts, the hatrack beside the front door, and my favourite place of all – the back of the neck of the skinny and trembling six-pound female rat terrier my mother had named Black Jet.

On weekends, I asked Daddy to drive me from pharmacy to toy store to department store, where I collected all *The Man from U.N.C.L.E.* accoutrements I could find – trading cards, magazines, books, guns, badges, walkie-talkies, LP records.

The Man from U.N.C.L.E. was last shown on NBC on 15 January 1968, my sixteenth birthday. To me, its passing was a major event. I had no friends, only Napoleon Solo books, magazines and the now darkened television. I had quit going to the movies.

I was five feet tall, weighed sixty-three pounds, and felt powerless and miserable. For my birthday present, hoping to capture The Power that Agent Solo had, that James Bond had, that all my Supermen had, I asked Daddy for karate lessons. The instructor we chose didn't look like Bond or Superman; he was short, Italian, overweight, and by day worked as a hairdresser. But Daddy religiously drove me to karate class, and I worked as hard as a sixty-three-pound runt could – punching and kicking the air in front of other skinny kids for an hour and a half four nights a week, sweating and hurting under fluorescent lights that made my skin look splotched and blue.

Workouts stimulated my appetite and my confidence. I began to dress spiffy and made friends. Girls took interest, but I was scared of them. 'Kid Karate' they called me in my junior yearbook. The year before no one had signed my annual and the few guys who'd talked to me had nicknamed me 'Foetus'.

During karate class, the fat hairdresser/instructor told us of great spiritual powers he possessed, and about Japanese gents who catch arrows in midflight, punch through watermelons, chew and swallow glass, shatter concrete blocks with their foreheads, kill with a single, seemingly ordinary touch. Whenever Sensei was asked to demonstrate his skills, he gracefully declined, saying that The Secrets were too powerful to show to just anyone. I kept sweating and hurting and kicking and punching and sweating under the lights, hoping to become good enough to learn The Secrets.

And Sensei kept telling us his stories. The one about the shrivelled and blind Buddhist monk who lived near Kyoto, and who had fought in, and been the survivor of, over fifteen hundred one-on-one death matches. And the one about Count Kamakura, who had been blessed with the gift of The Iron Palm by one of the ancients. No one could survive one of Count Kamakura's Iron Palm strikes. And of immortal, invincible masters whose eyes radiated a strange white heat, and upon whom no one dared look.

I believed the stories. I needed to.

After a year and a half of blistering work, I was awarded a brown belt, the rank immediately below black. I'd finally reached puberty and had grown to be a five-foot-four-inch, eighty-five-pound stud. It was soon after that I was to learn one of The Secrets.

Not from my hairdresser/karate sensei, but from Alvin Lindsor.

Alvin was the second smallest kid at school. He weighed eighty-eight pounds and was two years younger than me, though we were in the same grade. He was a standout member of the varsity wrestling squad, he fought with the Gladiators Amateur Boxing Team, stole beer from 7-Elevens, and whupped up on bigger kids in his spare time.

The high school that Alvin and I attended, Mount Tabor, was an all-white school and the Winston-Salem/Forsyth County School Board's experiment in progressive education. Basic English, math and health classes were taught by television sets. Sports history was offered as an alternative to senior English. Troublemakers weren't kept after school in teachers' offices or classrooms. Minor offenders – those caught chucking spit wads at Mr Evans, the gay biology teacher, chomping gum in Mr Morris's English literature class, arriving tardy for Miss Ooten's homeroom, or hunkering over fifteen-year-old Julia 'Jugs' Jordan's forty-inch mammaries – would report to Detention Study Hall promptly at 3.15, where they'd spend the next sixty minutes. Detention Study Hall was housed in the cafeteria. Alvin and I were charter members.

DSH, as we habituals called it, was founded on the hopeful assumption that if strays were herded into a central pen where they'd be overseen by a single trail boss, cowfolks would be free to complete their chores unhampered. The reality was that DSH was run by the bulls.

I first suspected The Secret in DSH. It was a Monday afternoon in February 1971 and I was serving a sentence for refusing to change for PE. I was sleeping at the far end of a yellow Formica-topped table, and when I woke and looked up, Alvin, who'd been sitting near the opposite end when I'd gone to sleep, was standing over me, holding my open history book in front of my face. Spit was rolling from its pages.

He closed the book, laid it on the table, walked to his seat, slapped hands with a couple wrestler buddies and sat down beside Joe Stone. Stone was short and bunchy muscled and had the same burning steel-grey eyes I envisioned the great Japanese karate masters having. He was twenty-one years old and was in the eleventh grade. My sophomore year, when sitting beside Stone in DSH, he'd ripped a sleeve from my favourite alpaca sweater and cut a quarter-inch-deep hole in my back with his pocket knife, all for fun. It was stuff like that, and the magma in his eyes, that made most everybody think Stone was a genuine maniac.

Out of the corner of my eye I saw Stone pass Alvin something, maybe a note, under the table. Alvin rose from his seat and ambled over. I began to sweat. Stone was looking past Alvin and at me. There was a glint in his eyes.

Alvin glared down at me, then lowered his right hand to my

bony excuse for a left biceps, which he squeezed a little, before sliding it across the shoulder of my hard-starched, almost brand-new Beau Brummell shirt, and up to the collar, which he wrenched into a knot. I reached to straighten it. Alvin slapped down my hand.

'Hey, you, you fuckin' Foetus, you. You got a lotta people fooled, actin' like you got some karate corncob stuck up your ass.' He thrust a jagged, bitten fingernail a few inches from my nose. 'Tomorrow, I'm gonna make you eat shit off that corncob, turdface.'

The teacher in charge of DSH didn't look up from papers he was grading. Alvin's friends laughed. Long, high, cackling, Southern laughter. There was something cold in the sound. Something that made my arms and legs feel frozen stiff to the ground.

I skipped first period the next morning. When I walked into homeroom, everyone was talking about the inevitable 'War of the Midgets'. At Mount Tabor, Miller–Lindsor would be as much the Fight of the Century as the Muhammad Ali–Joe Frazier bout that would take place in two weeks. Most students and even some teachers were placing bets on who'd win. Legend had it that Mr Cole, the wrestling coach, had twenty dollars on Alvin. Supposedly, so did Mr Bardy, the principal, who'd been a Golden Gloves boxer. Fourteen-year-old Batman, Green Hornet and James Bond fans were betting their quarters on me.

To get out of second-period study hall, I volunteered to deliver mimeographed copies of the list of absentees to teachers. Alvin and my sister were in the same Spanish class. Carol was sitting close to the front of the room; Alvin was on the next to last row, using his hands to play the drum solo from 'Wipe Out' on his desktop. When I passed him on the way to Miss Rapley's desk, some guy I didn't know, who was sitting next to Carol, yelled, 'There's that Karate Kid Miller Alvin's gonna beat crap out of.'

'Alvin couldn't beat me with a baseball bat,' I said almost instantly and very boldly, not only in defence of my pride and my family's, but in defence of the Japanese martial arts.

Guys laughed and made oohing sounds and somebody behind Alvin pushed his shoulders, prodding him on. I left the room, closing the door behind me.

I didn't go to school the next two days. Usually, when I skipped class I stayed in the building, creeping down the halls from one bathroom to the next, combing my hair and throwing hand strikes at my reflection in the mirrors above the sinks.

This time was different. I had a purpose. I pretended to be sick until Daddy left the house, then I got out of bed and worked out hard both days – and then both nights in Sensei's class – looking forward to the excellent opportunity Alvin had given me to showcase my rarefied abilities.

Tiger Claws, Dragon Rakes, Dream Fists, Sleeping Hands swirl like exploding skyrockets seen through a mist. Prisms of light leap effortlessly from my fingertips. Alvin falls before me and is grateful to have received a lesson in the fistic mysteries from his obvious superior.

Friday morning, I dressed in the trousers to my grey pinstripe suit and took extra time combing my hair so I'd look pretty for the fight. Daddy drove Carol and me to school. He let us out at the entrance and Carol went on ahead. An 'honour guard' of wrestlers and football players appeared from wherever they'd been waiting. They escorted me to Alvin, who was standing with a large pack of friends just inside the doorway.

I cocked my head to the side and put on my very best swagger for him. He sneered at me. 'Good mornin', faggot,' he spat. 'How come you never go out with no wimmin? You like men better, don't you, faggot.'

Before I could answer, he slapped me, hard, on the left cheek. My glasses flew from my face and ricocheted with a hollow metal sound off the row of lockers behind me.

I felt The Secret then, first in my stomach, next in my throat, but I pretended it wasn't there and shoved it down to my belly. 'Hey, man, not in here,' came a voice from some-where. 'Take him to the parking lot.'

Someone passed me my glasses. I put them on; they were lopsided. I remember floating out the door and across the asphalt, feeling the crowd grow around us. Alvin led me to the far end of the lot and up a grassy hill, where we stopped in front of a stand of scrub pines. I glanced behind me at the sea of people. All 2,000 Mount Tabor students, and their parents, had to be. I handed my glasses to a stranger. Jesus, what a bunch of faces. 'Break his ribs, Alvin.' Faces, full with a mean kind of joy.

I lowered myself into the deep, strong, bent-legged horse stance I'd practised for what had seemed endless hours in karate class (legs so far spread it looked as if I was trying to straddle the Pacific Ocean), and chambered both fists in the inverted *hachiji-dachi* position on the waist, elbows flat against the sides, chest thrust out, neck high and rigid, exactly the way Sensei had taught.

Alvin stared at me incredulously, until he realised I intended to fight from that stance. 'You gonna try'n kick me, pussy?' he said, smiling. He tucked his chin in next to his shoulder and raised both fists to ear level. 'Only girls and faggots kick each other,' he said, laughing.

He took two steps to the left and I turned with him, determined to face him no matter where he moved. He pushed an open palm into my nose, pulled it back. I kept both fists at my sides. He slapped me across the mouth with an open-handed jab, then another. I tried to deflect the second blow with the looping outside *age-uke* block; I was too stiff and too slow. He jabbed me again, close-fisted, and hooked off it. The punches didn't hurt, only numbed my face. I kept both fists chambered at the waist. Alvin slid two more jabs into my chin; my head twice slammed the back of my shoulders. He laughed again. Much of the crowd laughed with him. Their laughter thundered over me. Soon I was lost in the thunder.

Alvin tackled me at the waist, jumped on to my chest, pinning my arms, and punched both sides of my face. I felt the first shot bounce my head off the grass to the left, the second one to the right, before I managed to yank my arms free and grab his wrists, which I held, white-knuckled, until somebody screamed, 'Teacher.'

Alvin sprang from my chest and shape-shifted into the crowd. The guy holding my glasses put them on my face, pulled me to my feet, told me to run. I stumbled into the pines, still reeling in the thunder, until Mr Evans retrieved me and led me to the principal's office. Swimmy headed, I told Mr Bardy I thought Joe Stone had maybe offered Alvin some money to start the fight. He gave Alvin three licks with a wooden paddle, summoned Stone, told me to go to class. I left the building and walked home.

When Daddy came in from work, he took one look at me and said, 'Don't take an ass-kickin again, son. Even if you have to pick up a stick and crack 'em in the head with it.'

I promised I wouldn't.

That night, lying in bed, staring up into the dark with my face throbbing like I had a blown-up balloon lodged in each cheek, I recognised that in the two years I'd attended karate class, not once had anyone fought. Not once had anyone made contact with anything solid. Not once had I punched or kicked anything other than air and dreams.

The next day at school, Batman fans and my friends asked why I hadn't kicked Alvin or punched him back. I shrugged. How could I tell them I didn't know how.

I never returned to fat hairdresser/Sensei's karate class. And it wasn't long after my fight with Alvin that kids at school started calling me Foetus again. The next fall I transferred from Mount Tabor to a school on the other side of town.

ELLEN'S, DECEMBER 1971

Triad Style, 3 November 1996.

A long scene from this story also appears in The Tao of Bruce Lee. *The reason: 'Ellen's' was originally part of that book. The first draft of* The Tao of Bruce Lee *was 400 pages, which I edited to half that length. (Lee came and went in an eye blink; a book that can be read in one or two sittings seemed most appropriate.) I still like that first version best – 'Ellen's' is indicative of much of the writing that was cut – and I hope to eventually publish the book in a longer form.*

IN 1971, I was a senior at R.J. Reynolds High School in Winston-Salem, North Carolina. Reynolds was named after ol' Richard J. himself, the dead founder of the tobacco company that was the chief source of jobs in town. I was supposed to have graduated from another high school the year before but had been too busy sleeping with my head on my desk to get through remedial English.

I was five-foot-four, weighed eighty-six pounds, and was too scared of girls to talk to them. They weren't exactly pining their lives away over me, anyway, though I drove the hottest ride at school: a three-year-old, turquoise-coloured, 327/four-barrel Camaro with only 12,000 miles on the odometer. I washed the Camaro twice a week, every week, spent an hour or so cleaning the interior each time it was washed, and I waxed it every second week. Its black vinyl interior always shone. The turquoise paint beaded water better than anybody else's car I knew. At night, even when it wasn't raining, the Camaro looked wet under the city lights. Everybody wanted to ride in my Camaro. Even guys who didn't like me. And I didn't mind giving anybody rides. But I wouldn't let anyone use the ashtrays and everyone had to wipe their feet before they could place them on the floor mats. At least I pretended I could make them do those things. Even if I did need a three-inch-thick seat cushion to see over the steering wheel.

The first day at Reynolds, Marty Barkman (who'd offered to give me a dollar a week for rides) and I were heading up from the parking lot to the main classroom building when I saw her standing about fifty yards in front of us talking with a couple girls. Her hair was black and lustrous as pitchblende and it shimmered in the sun that morning when she pulled it behind her ears and it tumbled across her shoulders and down her back to just above her bottom.

Marty lit a Winston cigarette, left it dangling out of the corner of his mouth, sneaked up behind the girl and pinched her, sort of soft, kind of hard, right under where her hair had stopped growing. She jumped, he grabbed her about the waist with both hands and, grinning, said, 'Hey, sweet britches, where you been hidin'? Been lookin' for you all summer.'

I stood behind him and coveted his hands and how comfortable they seemed touching her. I'm pretty sure I was leering at her the same way a ten-year-old might. She had shining bronze skin and was about an inch or so taller than me; she had very long legs and a high, firm bum. I'm sure now that this was the first girl's bum I had noticed.

'Marty, aren't you ever going to leave me alone?' she said as she turned to face him. Then she smiled and said, 'Why don't you introduce me to your friend?' And then and there, my legs just about fell out from under me. Her eyes were cobalt; not grey, not blue, but silver. And they gave her a

143

powerful yet delicate presence. They were different from, better than, anyone's I'd ever seen.

'Oh . . . that's only Foetus. He gives me rides and buys me beer. Would you believe – this little shit's already nineteen?'

She scowled at Marty. 'What's your real name?' she said to me.

'Davis,' I answered, hoping she wouldn't hear my voice tremble, but thinking I'd better tell her before Marty had a chance to admit he didn't know. 'Davis Worth Miller,' I said.

'Davis,' she said in a way I'd never heard my name pronounced. 'Davis Miller,' she repeated. And she smiled at me again. She was the only person other than family and teachers who had called me Davis or Miller in a very long while. To everyone else I was 'Foetus' or 'Pissant' or 'Mouse' or 'Tadpole' or 'Squirt' or 'Shrimp' or 'Amoeba' or something besides me.

'What's your name?' I asked, struggling to get out the words.

'Ellen Rumfree,' she told me. 'Kind of boring, huh?' I said I didn't think so.

For the next week I couldn't work up nerve to talk to Ellen other than to say hello in the halls. But I found out what I could about her from Barkman on the way to Reynolds in the mornings. 'That bitch,' he said. 'Took her to the prom, figurin' I'd get me some. Cranford's parents were out of town and he said it was OK to use their bedroom. I'm puttin' my best moves on her when she sits up and starts laughin'. Goddamn bitch.'

Barkman told me Ellen was a junior and she wasn't very popular at RJR. She had friends, but not many. 'Mostly spaceheads,' Barkman said. 'She reads books. Not the fun kind about white ladies spreadin it for slaveboys, or diet books, or ghosts scarin' the bejesus out of somebody, or somethin' else normal like that for women to read. But hard shit like you're supposed to read in English – Shakespeare and all those other dead old farts. Even poetry. Can you believe it?' He made a face like he'd swallowed something big and sour. 'And she listens to real strung-out music. Ever heard of some Negro jazz-ass named the Loneliest Monk? Me, neither.'

At the beginning of lunch period a few days later, I was opening my car door as Ellen came bounding my way with a smile splashed across her face. Her hair was vibrating with each step she took; her breasts bounced in her white, rainbow-emblazoned T-shirt. Barkman had talked about what giant tits she had for a girl so thin, but to tell the truth, I hadn't noticed. My hormones didn't know enough about female anatomy to tell big ones from small.

'Davis Miller,' she said, the music still in the words. 'Would you carry me to lunch? I don't have room for me in my car.' She pointed at a sky-blue Pinto parked two spaces to the left and in front of mine and, when I managed to pull my eyes from hers, I saw why. She had five girls wedged on to the back seat and four more sardined together up front.

She walked to her car and handed the keys to the clunky blonde behind the wheel. 'We'll meet you at the Triangle,' she said.

All the way up Stratford Road, I didn't say a word. My hands were sweating so bad I could hardly keep them on the wheel. As I was letting Ellen out of the car, I made up a lie to avoid eating with her. I told her I'd better study for my Scholastic Aptitude Test.

Although I couldn't work up the nerve to talk to her, I began thinking about Ellen much of the time and even started going to school more often, not because I wanted to learn anything, but because I wanted to see her in the halls between classes and I figured I'd better try to get a diploma sometime this century.

For more than a year, I'd been trying to join the Polish Drinking Team, a fraternal and elitist group of ballplayers and wrestlers founded and led by Steve Romanosky and Sam Wesolowsky, both of whom had been born to Russian parents. Romo and Weso were renowned for leading each other around on all fours on a dog's leash and for barking and growling at women they'd pass in the halls at school or at bars and fast-food places.

The second weekend of October, Weso and Romo asked me for a ride to the football game so they could get good and juiced without worrying which of them would drive. I thought football was the dumbest sport going, all those fat-asses standing out in the light for everybody to see, wearing all those fat-ass pads and stupid uniforms and helmets and a ball and rules and shit. But everybody at Reynolds went to the games, and I was sure that meant Ellen, too.

The night before, we made a couple gallons of Purple Jesus and stored them in the trunk of the Camaro. Sitting in geometry, I could see them waiting for us, ripening and getting righteously toxic.

I washed and waxed the Camaro after school and spent three whole dollars filling up with gas. It was grey and cold that Friday, and clouds were round and rolling like ones you'd expect to see in *The Ten Commandments*. Just the right clouds and weather for football, even if I did hate the stupid fucking game.

Weso and Romo got wasted before we made it to the stadium. But I wanted my head clean and clear in case I should get up the nerve to talk to Ellen. We parked the car and moved off behind the stadium, away from the lights and into a stand of scraggly pines and dogwoods. The patch of woods was cold. The smell of wet fallen leaves enveloped us. We quickly found a place where we couldn't see the parking lot and where there were a bunch of ground-out cigarette butts at the base of the fence. When I'd climbed about halfway up, I noticed that Romo wasn't with us. I turned and looked for him and couldn't see through the trees. I jumped from the fence and stepped out from the woods into salmon-pink light from the big fluorescents.

There he was, about fifty yards from the Camaro, in the middle of a shining circle of shattered glass where nobody'd parked. Around him stood a gaggle of ten or so black kids who looked to be twelve to fourteen years old. And Romanosky was in some sort of pseudo-karate stance, one fist fully extended at shoulder height, the other inverted on the hip. And he was making some kind of dumb screeching noise and was hopping up and down like a radioactive rooster.

I sprinted across the parking lot to help. I heard Weso's big feet clunking up behind. 'Hey, cuz, what's goin' on?' I asked the tallest and blackest of the blacks, the one who seemed to be the leader.

He ignored me. 'Here comes your white-ass cavalry, Mr Karate Man,' he said to Romo, sporting the coldest grin I had ever seen. We were only a couple miles from the downtown Reynolds plants. The too-sweet, dusky smell of cured tobacco was in the air. I pulled at Steve's sleeve. His longish cheeks looked tight and sunken. One of them trembled every few seconds. Although it was cold enough to see his breath in the air, his reddish hair was stuck by sweat to his temples and his skin looked clammy.

'Come on, Romo, let's go,' I said. 'Come on, now, don't nobody want no trouble.' I felt glass crunch under my shoes.

And Crowblack hit me on the stomach with a bag of nickels he'd been hiding somewhere. I heard it jangle and knew what it was. But it didn't hurt. I guess he didn't know how to angle a punch.

Why'd you do that? I wanted to ask. Look at my clothes. Hear my voice. Go check out my car. Can't you tell how hip I am? Don't look at my face. That ain't me. Can't you tell I'm a lot like you? Can't you see these clowns use me, too?

And Crowblack tried to hit me again. Before he got his bag-slow fist halfway round, I stabbed him, flat on the bridge of the nose, with two hard left jabs. Where had those come from? Had I really thrown them? The punches had come out so smooth and easy, just like on TV and in the movies. And then, Crowblack was lying down. And there was blood everywhere; everywhere there was blood. From out of his nostrils, around his mouth, down his neck and shirt, it flowed, and there was a little puddle of it on the asphalt and glass beside his head.

I looked for Weso: he was running for the car. Romo still stood beside me, off to the left, in that stupid karate stance. 'Go ahead,' another black kid was saying, 'try some of your ka-raw-ti-shit.' No one realised I'd hit their friend.

I grabbed Romo by the arm and pulled him hard, spinning him toward me. 'The car,' I said, 'go to the car,' and I dug my feet in and took off running. Steve beat me to the Camaro and I threw him the keys. He unlocked the door on the passenger's side and he and Weso slid on to the bucket seat. One of them opened my door for me.

I jumped behind the wheel, we locked both doors and tried to tear out of there. A big black Buick pulled in the way and blocked the exit. Another dark car fell in behind.

I couldn't back up, couldn't go forward. There I sat with my foot on the brake while the hive of dirty, sweaty thirteen-year-olds descended on my clean, mean, cool-blue ride. They swarmed all around, whirling up and down on the fenders, smearing street-soiled fingers all over my fresh-Windexed windows. And then Crowblack was there, blood pouring from his nose, green shining shards of glass sticking out of his cheek, standing there beside my door. And he had an empty Rebel Yell bottle coiled in his fist, the bottle not yet a part of the hand, his hand still young and mouldable-looking, looking like it should be holding a couple slices of Sunbeam bread with peanut butter chunked up in between.

He swung and broke the bottle on the window next to my face. I jumped and put my hands beside my head, but the window didn't shatter. 'There's some cops, over there,' Weso yelled. I looked where he pointed. Not a hundred yards away, there they were, two of them, both white, directing traffic with big orange flashlights, looking as bored as the kids in remedial English class. I blew the horn once, twice, held it down. Crowblack was kicking my door. Two other kids were pounding on the hood. One cop finally looked up, said something at

148

his partner, pulled out his stick and jogged methodically toward us. I saw a lot of legs dart past, turned and watched thirteen-year-olds fly off in some ten different trajectories. The Buick in front of us finally moved. I pulled on to the street, then over to the kerb. I climbed out and told my story to the second cop. He looked sleepy and kept directing traffic.

'Well, what do you expect me to do, son?' he said in his best self-contained cop voice. 'Something like this happens most every weekend.'

Yeah, I thought, but you're missing the point. The point is it doesn't happen to me and my car – and you're not a very nice guy to be a peace officer. 'Look at these giant dents all over my car,' is all I said.

'Go on about your business, son,' he answered.

To calm down, we drove around, each of us taking a couple dips into the vat of PJ. When we figured the game was over, we headed for Staley's, a burger joint that had been the post-game hangout for at least a thousand years.

About halfway there, Weso reached across Romo and clapped me on the shoulder. 'Goddamn, Davis, didn't know you had it in you,' he said. I smiled. He'd called me 'Davis'. Not 'Foetus'. Not 'Pissant'. Not 'Mouse'. Not 'Tadpole'. Maybe Weso wasn't such a bad guy, after all.

'Didn't know you'd been takin' judo. What belt you got, anyway – black?'

I didn't bother to tell them what I'd done wasn't any kind of Asian martial art. Or that it had happened by accident. I'd quit thinking about what they said or the words that came from my mouth. I was dreaming what it would be like at Staley's, hoping she'd be there. There, her hair and eyes all incandescent. Smiling a sympathetic smile and giving me soulful, understanding looks when I told her what happened to the Camaro.

And she was at Staley's. She was standing near the back with a bunch of girls. Sweet freedom. Standing right there just as plain as day. Free at last. And there were no guys anywhere near. Thank God, Almighty, free at last.

Steve and Sam and I took a seat close to the door, but they kept getting up to tell the story to everyone in the room. As they made their way round, hands kept coming over to the table, and smiling faces, beaming faces, wanting to offer congratulations, and faces full and wide with some semblance of pride. They'd finally accepted me. They were all impressed.

Everyone was impressed. Except Ellen. Hands kept slapping my shoulders and she was staring at me from across the room and looking disappointed.

And more guys kept wanting to shake my hand. I was talking and smiling and feeling good about being the hero and I looked up from the table and she was gone.

The next day, after washing and waxing the Camaro (which made me feel even worse about the craters in the door and on the hood), I drove to Reznick's Records at Thruway Shopping Center and picked up all three James Taylor eight-tracks and a copy of *Abbey Road*, hoping Ellen would listen to them with me and be surprised to find out that I was sensitive after all, when I finally found the nerve to ask her if she wanted a ride to lunch.

The day after Christmas she surprised me by stopping by the house. I ran outside when I realised her car had pulled into the driveway. 'Just wanted to see how you're doing,' she said. 'Gotten your car fixed?'

'About a month ago,' I said.

'Good. Take me for a ride and we'll listen to this.'

From the rear pocket of her jeans, she pulled a red- and green-wrapped package exactly the size of an eight-track. I tore off the paper. It was the new Simon and Garfunkel, *Bridge Over Troubled Waters*.

'God, Ellen, I don't have any gas in the car,' I lied. 'And I've got to go to my grandmother's and open presents.'

As much as I wanted to cruise around with Ellen and as good as it felt that she'd bought me a present, I was scared that just by being in the same car with her, my hands would sweat so much we'd have a wreck.

'Maybe sometime soon,' she said.

When she left, I got in the Camaro and drove fast and hard out to the Yadkin River, taking the long way around, tearing down curving country roads at eighty miles an hour, wasting a half-tank of gas before coming home.

Two days before New Year's and four days before time to go back to school, Ellen called and said Scott Bauer was having a party. His parents were out of town and she asked if I'd go with her. I didn't know what to say.

'When?' I finally asked.

'Tonight,' she said.

Then she squealed and it startled me and I asked what was wrong.

'Wrong? Nothing's wrong. It's snowing. Look, Davis.'

I parted the window blinds and it sure was, all right. It was coming down real thick and smooth. I should've noticed before, I thought. It's been quiet for some time, now. And the road in front of the house is never quiet unless it snows.

Well, what do you know. Christmas and New Year's and a party and Ellen and snow. Fireplaces and Mom and Dad and turkey and eggnog and Irving Berlin and friends, drinks, parties, and clean, white, silent snow. And Ellen.

Sure, I'd love to go, I heard someone say. I'll meet you there. After Ellen hung up, I realised the agreeing voice had been mine.

By seven o'clock, four inches were on the ground. Scott's house was on the hill above Daddy's and I tugged on a pair of corduroys, borrowed Daddy's thick socks, pulled on my leather jacket, fur-lined gloves, and a grey wool golf cap, and began the climb.

When I got to Scott's, Ellen was waiting. And there was good music.

Good, warm music. Sweet, soft, soul sounds. Little Anthony and the Imperials; Marvin Gaye and Tammi Terrell; Curtis Mayfield and the Impressions. And the walls were made of old, dark brick. Someone passed me a steaming hot toddy. I was still wearing gloves and she took my sheathed hand and we went and sat on a sofa by ourselves.

'Got tired of waiting for you to ask me out,' she said. 'Or at least to talk to me.'

I finished the drink, said, 'Excuse me,' got up, found the refrigerator, and grabbed a beer. I sat down beside her.

'What are you waiting for?' she said after an hour or so, and she smiled a kind of smile I hadn't seen before and raised one eyebrow. 'There's no need to be so shy with me.'

I smiled, too, and popped another top.

'There's nothing to be scared of. I won't bite. And even if I do,' she paused, carefully timing each word that would follow, 'it'll be in a friendly kind of way.'

I turned up the beer. That's exactly what I was scared of. Bad as I wanted it – and her – I was afraid I didn't have the teeth to bite back.

I'm at my old elementary school. On the playground. Riding the Whirl-Me. I lay my head back and watch the sky roll around me. I get dizzy. I look down. And she's there, Ellen, and she's naked and wet, like she stepped from a stream, and she's standing in front of the pines. Her hair flows down the sides of her face. The Whirl-Me stops. I stare. Her skin is luminous with water and suntan and ancestry. She's standing, legs slightly apart, hands poised on her hips, waiting for me. Standing like the girls in Playboy. *Small beads of water reflect light from the V of black hair down there. I step off the Whirl-Me. My mouth feels numb. I run my tongue across my gums. I don't feel any teeth. I reach in: they all fall out. I see them lying in the sand. I look up. And Ellen is gone.*

*

I sat the empty can on the table. Someone handed me another. I finished it and took a long bubbling hit off Marty's bottle of J & B.

Ellen was still sitting next to me and she was talking and I had got myself all comatosed and didn't even know it. And then I realised she'd placed one palm high on my right thigh and was lightly stroking my left shoulder with her other hand. And she'd been doing it for a while. Something fluttered in my belly.

'I'll be back,' I said.

'Where are you going?' she said, her voice drifting in from another galaxy.

I moved across the room in a slow, wandering dance. Then I was outside, not feeling the cold, my legs falling under me, but not completely giving way. I stumbled to the side of the yard and hung myself across a picket fence and began heaving, my head bobbing up and down, a low wailing going off in my skull, not feeling the cold, not feeling anything at all, and then feeling her hands again, cupped soft yet firm around my waist.

Then the light was white and I was upstairs under the covers in one of the beds and I wasn't wearing any clothes except for underwear. I had been tucked in on both sides like when I was a kid, warm and snug and safe, and Ellen was lying next to me, fully clothed and on top of the covers, her body curved around mine. I felt her hair on my chest. There was a cool, wet washcloth being pressed to my face. And she said, You really shouldn't drink like that. She said, You don't have to be so stupid. Call me tomorrow, she said. Then she was gone. I struggled up, found my clothes where she'd left them neatly folded at the foot of the bed, and I slid back down the hill through the snow, to Daddy's.

The first day back at school, I was finally admitted to the Polish Drinking Team. Romo and Weso presented me with an official jersey at a special meeting that took place in the hospitality room of the Schlitz brewery out off Highway 109.

The shirt was black; my name and title had been stencilled on in big yellow block letters above my official number, '00'. 'PISSANT-SKI, DRILL INSTRUCTOR', the shirt read. I tried it on. It was only about a hundred sizes too big.

Every Friday, I proudly wore the jersey as if it were a letter sweater. PDT meetings took place on Friday nights at Sam's Tavern on the Green. Soon it was March and time to order caps and gowns. A form was given to seniors requesting the correct spelling of names for graduation programmes. I printed mine as 'Davis Worth Miller III'. The 'III' part was a complete lie. But I thought it made me sound cool and important. Made me special. And in the area provided for honours and activities, I listed myself as drill instructor for the Polish Jerk-Off Team. When Daddy asked to attend my graduation, I told him I'd decided not to go. But I didn't tell anybody at Reynolds.

The next time I saw Ellen when I couldn't avoid her, it was on a Friday afternoon in April, the week the cherry trees blossomed. There'd be a basketball game that night. I didn't want to attend the sixth-period pep rally, so I sneaked off and was sitting on a hill out back. A shadow moved up from behind. I turned. She was wearing a blue flannel shirt that set off her eyes perfectly. A couple buttons had been left undone. Her breasts swayed under the soft fabric. Although it was eighty degrees, my shirt was starched to the max and I was wearing a red alpaca sweater and, as always, the golf cap that gave me a casual look.

We talked for a while over the noise echoing from the auditorium and soon she'd kicked off her shoes in the grass and I stood and we began to move away from school and the thunder and toward the aisle of cherry trees. Suddenly we were stepping among fallen petals. She asked what I had planned for Saturday night. 'I don't know,' I answered. 'The usual, I guess.'

'Well, if you're not doing anything, why don't you take me to a movie?'

I didn't answer. I wanted to, but couldn't. I reached for her hand, took it. I looked at our hands together, the differences in colour, her fingers longer than mine. How strong and alive and gentle was her touch and how I wished I could wrap myself around her, how I wanted to crawl up inside her, wanted to breathe the air she breathed, wanted to see the world she saw. How simple, purposeful and sacred everything became for that instant. Then my palm began to sweat and the moment had gone on too long. I let go and we walked silently back to the auditorium through the blanket of blossoms, she apparently realising I'd never ask her. But how could I tell her I'd never been out with a girl, that I'd never done anything with anybody. I knew she'd laugh at me if I did. Or, even worse, she'd totally ignore me.

I'm drunk. Stumbling down the middle of the first-floor hall, outside and between the girls' and boys' restrooms.

Ellen walks past; I try to say hi, but my tongue's too thick for words. She doesn't see me, anyway. She's staring straight at me, but can't see me. I look at my trousers, at my zipper. My thing is hanging out, loose and limp and waggling. I lurch into a restroom, wanting to hide. I stumble to the back, find the latrine – the large, old, open, concrete kind – and I piss. When I'm finished, I tuck it back in my trousers and move dizzily for the door, through a crowd that has entered behind me. It takes a few seconds to notice that the people are very small boys and their mothers. What are these women doing here? I wonder. When I exit and look at the sign over the door, I realise I'd entered the wrong room. GIRLS, the sign reads.

I told myself I'd wait until September to ask her out, when the other guys went away to college. That fall, I'd see Ellen from a distance every once in a while, at Staley's after a ball game or passing her car. Twice, she stopped by after school to say hello.

Every day, I drove the Camaro past Ellen's house five, sometimes ten, times, all on Daddy's gas money. First thing when I woke, I'd pull out of the driveway and head for Highway 158. If it was around lunchtime, I might hear the 12.30 freight train moaning up ahead, and I'd go left, following the sound and the tracks up The Strip, past tobacco and cotton and corn fields, thundering around old slow-going Ford and Chevy pick-ups, up where 158 becomes Stratford Road and kudzu vines stop creeping so close to the road and you can't smell them any more when they die in the fall, past all the spots where white kids cruise on weekend nights – Putt-Putt, where I'd sometimes pass the train, and the Triangle Drive-In – and on into town, right on by Krispy Kreme's shining green and red neon sign imperatively flashing *Hot Doughnuts NOW* as if the words really meant something, as if they *had* to mean something, and past fat-ass Lincolns and Cadillacs parked at Food Fair and at Davis Department Store over at Thruway and the fat-ass old women who drove the Caddies and who struggled to open and close their fat-ass car doors.

Don't none of the people in this town know nothin' about nothin', I'd think, and they don't want to know nothin'. But I don't know nothin either, and don't have nowhere to go, and don't know how to get there even if I did.

On up to Five Points I'd head, where I'd bear left at Reynolds Drive, starting in nice and slow and speeding up as I got close to Ellen's house, mashing the accelerator to the floor and not looking left or right (but still wanting to seem real loose and relaxed) as the Camaro howled past her driveway.

Five, maybe ten times a day I'd pass her house, hoping, longing, dreaming she'd be outside and I could stop and say how happy I was to have bumped into her and, 'Wouldn't you like to dance with me tonight?' or, 'Would you like to go to a movie?' and, of course, she was never sitting on the kerb waiting for me and even if she had been, I couldn't have made myself stop.

Between drives by Ellen's, until it turned cold, I'd lie in the sun and drink beer and listen to Isaac Hayes eight-tracks. I'd walk back to Silas Creek and stare at the water and try to imagine Ellen and me in rolled-up jeans splashing about just like in Salem cigarette ads.

The next time I heard of Ellen, it was the week before Christmas 1976. I'd recently moved back to my father's house. I'd been staying up in the mountains and down on the coast, gaining height and weight and confidence and finally finding myself a life. I was teaching martial art and exploring ambitions of trying to become a world-champion kick-boxer and a novelist. I planned to marry a girl who had convinced me to study creative writing at a university.

I saw Marty Barkman at Thruway Shopping Center, where I'd gone to look at diamonds. We talked about people we'd known in high school. He told me Ellen was in her senior year at Meredith College, and she was going out with Frank Davis, a former PDT member (Davis-ski, read his sweatshirt). I hoped I'd see her before Lyn and I got married, believing she'd be impressed with the person I was becoming.

One morning right after Christmas, I sat down to breakfast with the newspaper. And there it was, right at the top of page two – the night before, out on US Highway 421 close to North Wilkesboro, while driving Frank Davis's car home from a party, twenty-one-year-old Ellen Rumfree had been killed in a head-on collision with a drunk driver.

We tell each other we wish we could go back and redo things. I don't have to tell you what I wish I'd done. You already know.

The more fortunate among us have opportunities to name buildings and fellowships after our dead, hoping to immortalise them and maybe exorcise guilt over not having given enough of ourselves while they were alive. I recognise that this final thing I need to say sounds big-hokey, but I don't particularly give a shit: this story is the present I wish I'd given Ellen Rumfree for Christmas my senior year in high school in 1971.

THE BEST FATHER

Candis, May 1998.

THE VOICE ON the answering machine is so low and broken I'm not sure I'd recognise the caller if he didn't tell who he was.

'Son, this is your dad,' the voice says slowly, falling off near the end of the sentence. 'Give me a call when you get in.'

Instead of calling back, I drive straight to his house. He's in his easy chair across from the TV, a John Wayne western shooting up the room. He's dressed like he's ready to go to work, wearing a pair of chocolate dress slacks and a checked short-sleeve shirt.

'It's beautiful outside,' I say. 'Feels like fall.'

'Every time I've gone to the hospital,' says my father, 'it's been weather like this. So clear it hurts your eyes. Clear as the mornin' the space shuttle blew up.'

I eye Daddy hard. I've never seen anyone look the way he does right now. Shocked to the marrow. In downright awe. Yet fallen into his body. And almost entirely resigned.

'Son, my chest hurts,' he says. Daddy never talks about how he feels. 'Don't want to go to the hospital. Don't want to die in no hospital.'

His matter-of-factness stuns me; I don't know what to say or do. So I laugh. 'You're not dying,' I say. 'You're fine.'

159

He moves to his desk and writes cheques for water and electric bills and for his charge cards. Like when I was a kid, he asks me to lick stamps and seal envelopes.

'Ambulances cost too much,' he says. 'You take me in.'

In the cardiac care unit, they stretch him out in bed in a hospital gown, hook him to a heart monitor and a couple other machines. His pulse is 118. That seems awfully high.

A red-haired nurse asks questions and writes answers. 'Are you a smoker?'

'Not any more,' answers my father.

'When did you stop?' she asks.

'This morning,' he says, and sort of laughs.

His questioner doesn't smile. She makes a note, pulls up the sheet, looks at Daddy's feet. 'How long they been swollen like this?' she says.

'I don't know,' he says. 'A while, I guess.'

I stare at his feet. They're dry, tightly swollen and painful looking, as swollen as latex gloves full of hot water. I wish I'd noticed before; I wish I'd known to notice.

'Mister . . . uh . . . Miller,' she says, looking for his name on her clipboard, 'tell me about your pain.'

'It's not pain. Not like when I had my heart attack and it felt like somebody sittin on my chest. Just tightness. That's all.'

Her pen moves across the paper. 'Are you an organ donor?'

When Daddy shakes his head and looks distressed, she asks, 'Do you want to donate your organs? At your age, your eyes probably aren't good any more, but there may be other parts somebody can use.'

At your age. This woman's got the worst bedside manner of all time. She's treating this fine man, Roy L. Miller, as if he's part of the machinery in this room. I look at Daddy; he seems shocked. I'm surprised, too. Mostly not by this woman's gall, but by the notion that my father could be too old to give away his parts.

*

Throughout the day Daddy is poked and prodded by a procession of nurses, medical students and residents. I pull a kind-acting doc to the side and tell him that Daddy believes he's dying. 'There's nothing to support that,' he says. 'His vital signs look great, his pulse is strong.'

I tell him I think Daddy may be depressed. 'It's helpful to know how patients feel,' he says, pushing his glasses further back on his nose. 'We'll talk with him. Tell him what we know. Build his confidence.'

I look at Daddy's watch. It's 9.25. I'm yawning full-bodied yawns and my stomach has been rumbling since before dark. Daddy tells me to go get dinner and some sleep.

'Do me a favour, Dave,' he says as I'm headed out the door. 'Don't tell your sister I'm in the hospital. I don't want to worry her.'

As I'm wolfing down a sandwich, Lyn calls from the beach, where she's taken the kids for Labour Day. 'Wanted to let you know we got here.'

'I don't want to alarm you,' I say, 'but Daddy's in the hospital. It's his heart. I think he's all right, but he says he's dying. You might want to come home early.'

The other end is silent, then: 'I'm sure he's OK,' Lyn says.

The doctors, the nurses, Lyn and me: no one feels Daddy's in trouble. That heart attack he had in the mid-seventies, what would anybody expect, raising a little shit like me. But I've got it together pretty good now. I'm becoming a fully actualised man. At last, I'll have time to spend with Daddy. That's the way the universe works. Live the right ways and you're rewarded.

'On Monday they'll give him a cath. See if he needs a bypass. But I think you might want to come home tomorrow.'

'You weren't upset when my father was in the hospital. You didn't go out of your way to see him.'

161

She's right: I didn't. When Lyn and I were dating, her parents said that at twenty-three, I was too old for her. I had no business bumming around the way I did. Kick-boxer. Whatever that was. Writer. You've got to be kidding. What kind of future could she possibly have with a flake like me?

'We knew your father needed a bypass,' I tell her. 'We don't know with Daddy.'

'He's OK,' she says, not dismissively, just convinced. 'The kids are having a great time. If there's an emergency, give me a call. Otherwise, we'll see you Sunday.'

Saturday. Daddy looks better. The heart monitor reads seventy-six. Yes. Much better.

I call Carol, feeling lucky to catch her during the holiday weekend. She asks why I didn't phone earlier. 'You know Daddy,' I say, 'always wanting to shield us from everything.'

Monday morning. Labour Day. Lyn and the kids got in from the beach last night. Lyn will visit Daddy on her morning work break, after his cath. This morning, he's quiet but holding himself with confidence, having been reassured by docs, nurses, Carol, me.

Carol and I cheer him off for his procedure. I ask if she'd like breakfast. We drive to a pancake place, Cloverdale Kitchen. When we come back about 9.15, a nurse says she's been looking for us. 'Your father had some trouble. He's asking for you.'

My legs go weak, but I run toward his cubicle. Ten feet away, I slow to a walk and force myself to look calm. He's cranked up in bed: transparent plastic draped about his head and torso, a thin, clear hose in each nostril. A wet sucking sound fills the room. I've never seen an oxygen tent, but I'm pretty sure that's what this is. I remember Daddy telling us about one they put our mother under, the day she died, in this hospital.

I ask Daddy how he's doing. He looks almost OK, a little

tired and scared. 'Better than an hour ago,' he says, his voice careful, intimate and amazed.

A handsome blond guy comes in and introduces himself as, 'Steve Mills, the cardiothoracic surgeon who supervised your cath.'

Dr Mills clears his throat and looks at my father. Then I get the answer to one of those questions I'm sure we all wonder about, though I'm certain we never want to know the answer. How would the doctor tell you that you were dying?

He does it this way: he looks terse, regretful, understanding, sympathetic, yet removed. It's exactly the way I envisioned it would be, but never expected to hear. It's all you could ask from a stranger.

'Mr Miller,' he says without having to look at a chart, 'three vessels supply blood to your heart. Two of them are blocked with plaque, the third is ninety-five per cent closed. And your heart muscle isn't working well. This is recent damage. We have several options – but no matter what we try, there's slim chance of success. Do you understand what I'm saying?'

'You're sayin' I'm between a rock and a hard place.'

'That's about it,' says Dr Mills.

I move to Daddy's side. And I hold my father's hand and stroke his hair, things I haven't done since I was twelve years old.

Ever since my mother's death, and the ways I shut down in reaction to it, Daddy's shielded me from every painful thing he could. Here, today, I've decided that no matter what, I'm going to stay with this, I'm not going to look the other way. It's not fair to Daddy to do anything less.

I work toward the courage to tell him what I've believed I'd have all the time in the world to say. 'You and I never tell each other how we feel,' I start, my voice maybe half steady. 'But I think I should say this – you've been the best father I could ever imagine having had.'

Then: my throat shuts tight. I can't utter one more word. Daddy starts to cry, as do I. He reaches to take me in his arms and to kiss me on the lips. We're stopped by the plastic tent. 'I've got things to tell you, too, son,' he says. 'But I just can't do it right now.'

You know what happens, but I'm going to show you some of it anyway.

Lyn takes off from work and comes to see Daddy, as do her parents. I ask my father if he'd like Johanna and Isaac to visit. He says we'll see how it goes.

Early afternoon, I'm alone with him as a nurse comes to check the medications in his IV. He closes his eyes. When he opens them, he asks the nurse for nitroglycerine.

'Have you had pain?' she says, turning her eyes to the monitor. Daddy's pulse is seventy-eight. Everything looks fine.

'You're getting nitro in your IV,' says the nurse. 'Are you having pain now?'

Daddy closes his eyes. 'I breathe better when I'm sittin' up. Will you put me up?'

The nurse looks at him, long, and looks at the monitor.

'I don't want to give you a hard time,' says my father, 'but if you don't put me up, I'm gonna climb out of this bed.'

Even now, Daddy's the manager, trying to take care of everything, wanting to make everything all right.

Trying not to appear hurried, the nurse leaves the cubicle. She returns with a young man in green scrubs, who doesn't say anything, just looks at the monitor.

I move beside Daddy and take his hand. The man in green puts Daddy down flat. Daddy closes his eyes and bears down so tight on his lips that they go white; he shakes his head, big and slow, from side to side. Daddy looks utterly innocent. He continues shaking his head, moving it with the bottomless disappointment of a child. I grit my teeth. Two more people enter the cubicle and hasten to Daddy's side. There's a hand gentle at the inside of my forearm, near the elbow. 'We need you to leave now,' comes a woman's voice, soft and level. She pulls the curtain closed behind me.

It's five hours before they let me in with Daddy. Carol, Lyn and I are taken to a waiting room, where we're told he's had a myocardial infarction and probably a stroke, that he's very near death. We take this in real smooth, like slowly swimming underwater in a deep, black pool.

There's no way to be prepared for what I find when I'm finally allowed into Daddy's space. When the plastic curtain is pulled back, Daddy has been replaced by a giant orange frog that looks like my father.

The frog's head has been thrown back at a horrible angle. Its neck is grotesquely oedematous, the right eye closed, the cornea of the unseeing left shudders electrically. Its mouth is as slack as a worn-out sock. The smell that fills this space has a more powerful presence than any other phenomenon in the room. It's the most real thing I've ever been around. In my whole life, nothing else has ever come close. Period.

I'm so in awe of the presence in the room that it's days, weeks, months before I know what to get mad about. When I do, I'm angry that I was disconnected from Daddy at a time of terrible intimacy, that I was rushed from his side, when no one had any right, legal or otherwise, to do so.

When I get the bill, there are ten pages of chemicals that were shot through his system during those last hours. I'm furious that Daddy was unintentionally tortured. And what I'd like to do is kick the gonads off the system that teaches people to treat human beings as mechanically as they do. And maybe I'd like to snatch the Big Ancient White Cat Himself off His mountain and knock the Holy Shit out of Him for designing it this way, or letting it be this way, or for not telling us why, or for something.

Or maybe it's the old concept of Mr White-Beard I'd like to snatch from the mountain.

Anyway, I hold Daddy's hand and talk with him. His

fingers constantly tremble, but when I tell him I love him, he seems to press his middle finger into the heart of my palm.

Daddy lets the world out of his lungs, at 8.25 a.m. on 6 September 1989. At the funeral, Carol reaches into the casket, tugs his gold watch from his wrist and places it on mine. It's an Elgin, given to him less than a year ago for forty years of service with the corrugated box company where he worked.

That night, I drive to the children's playground at Sherwood Forest Elementary School, where I attended third through sixth grades. A seesaw, sandbox, teeter-totter, a big set of swings. I take a seat on the middle swing, lay my head way back, try to look through the dull orange glow of city lights, searching for shapes in the clouds. I don't see any.

It's not at all like Hollywood, I think. You have memories, but not the big stuff, the events. You remember how, when you were little, he liked to drive in the rain and that he packed everybody in the car to head downtown in summer storms; how he blew his nose, the sound not so much of his voice as of his cough; that he always smiled with his mouth closed because he was embarrassed by his crooked teeth; the arc of his fingernails; the way he slurped his milk. Nothing dramatic.

And you start finding him in almost every personal gesture you thought was your own. Even the way I sign my name is like Daddy's. In junior high, I worked for hours to emulate his handwriting, not only so I could forge his name on my report card when I failed classes, but because his signature was so graceful, so very beautiful.

When I was small, maybe five or six, Daddy'd put me on the big swings and I'd get dizzy, feel sick; I'd be terrified. I'd cry and cry, really wail. Now I plant my feet in the sand and push back hard, kick my legs way up. I watch pines whisk past, then sand, then grass, pines, sand, grass. I go up and up. Pushing, pumping.

It's the only thing that makes any sense at all. Swinging on the big swings. Swinging hard. Just kick those legs up and pump for the sky.